Books are to be returned on or before
the last date below.

26 OCT 2006

**7 – DAY
LOAN**

WILEY SERIES
in
CHILD PROTECTION AND POLICY

Series Editor: Christopher Cloke,
NSPCC, 42 Curtain Road,
London EC2A 3NX

This NSPCC/Wiley series explores current issues relating to the prevention of child abuse and the protection of children. The series aims to publish titles that focus on professional practice and policy, and the practical application of research. The books are leading edge and innovative and reflect a multi-disciplinary and inter-agency approach to the prevention of child abuse and the protection of children.

This series is essential reading for all professionals and researchers concerned with the prevention of child abuse and the protection of children. The accessible style will appeal to parents and carers. All books have a policy or practice orientation with referenced information from theory and research.

SUPPORTING FAMILIES

Child Protection in the Community

Ruth Gardner

Royal Holloway College, London UK

JOHN WILEY & SONS, LTD

Telephone (+44) 1243 779777

Paperback edition first published January 2005

Email (for orders and customer service enquiries): cs-books@wiley.co.uk
Visit our Home Page on www.wileyeurope.com or www.wiley.com

This publication is designed to provide accurate and authoritative information in regard to the subject matter covered. It is sold on the understanding that the Publisher is not engaged in rendering professional services. If professional advice or other expert assistance is required, the services of a competent professional should be sought.

Other Wiley Editorial Offices

John Wiley & Sons Inc., 111 River Street, Hoboken, NJ 07030, USA

Jossey-Bass, 989 Market Street, San Francisco, CA 94103-1741, USA

Wiley-VCH Verlag GmbH, Boschstr. 12, D-69469 Weinheim, Germany

John Wiley & Sons Australia Ltd, 33 Park Road, Milton, Queensland 4064, Australia

John Wiley & Sons (Asia) Pte Ltd, 2 Clementi Loop #02-01, Jin Xing Distripark, Singapore 129809

John Wiley & Sons Canada Ltd, 22 Worcester Road, Etobicoke, Ontario, Canada M9W 1L1

Library of Congress Cataloguing-in-Publication Data

Gardner, Ruth (Mary Ruth)
    Supporting families : a professional guide / Ruth Gardner.
        p.   cm.—(Wiley series in child protection and policy)
    Includes bibliographical references and index.
    ISBN 0-471-49970-6
    1. Family services—Great Britain.   2. Problem families—Great Britain.   3. Child welfare—Great Britain.   4. National Society for the Prevention of Cruelty to Children.
I. Title.   II. Series.

    HV700.G7 G33   2003
    362.82′0941—dc21   2002027234

British Library Cataloguing in Publication Data

A catalogue record for this book is available from the British Library

ISBN 0-471-49970-6 (hbk)
ISBN 0-470-02302-3 (pbk)

Typeset in 10/12pt Palatino by TechBooks, New Delhi, India
Printed and bound in Great Britain by Antony Rowe Ltd, Chippenham, Wiltshire
This book is printed on acid-free paper responsibly manufactured from sustainable forestry in which at least two trees are planted for each one used for paper production.

CONTENTS

FOREWORD

This book, with which I am privileged to be associated, represents the first publication to derive from a very exciting partnership between the Department of Health and Social Care at Royal Holloway, London University, and the NSPCC. The NSPCC has funded, since 1998, a Senior Research Fellowship in the Department of Health and Social Care at Royal Holloway; Dr Ruth Gardner, the book's author, is the first incumbent of that post. This research partnership between NSPCC and Royal Holloway is a reflection of the commitment of NSPCC to evidence-based practice, and of its enthusiasm for evaluating NSPCC services within that research-focussed policy context. In addition, the partnership reflects NSPCC's determination to bring an external and, to the best of our ability, objective contribution to the task of evaluating its services.

In my view, it is particularly appropriate that the Fellowship has been linked to the NSPCC's Evaluation Department. This location gives an unambiguous message to service users and to staff about the centrality of the link between practice and evaluation. Research should be seen as a tool for good practice, not merely as an academic exercise whose findings will inform theory, may inform policy, but will rarely inform practice.

It is also appropriate that the focus of the study, on which this book is based, is NSPCC's Family Support activity. This is an area of the organisation's work that sometimes gets overshadowed by its image in the public mind as (only) a Child Protection Agency. As child care research has consistently demonstrated (including the overviews of research—*Children Act Now* and *Supporting Parents*), there is a close link between *Family Support* and *Child Protection*. In reality they occupy a common continuum along which parents, carers, and voluntary and statutory agencies strive to maximise the developmental welfare of children. Ruth's study has highlighted the complexity of the challenges faced by the NSPCC families and workers with whom she spoke. Their views and aspirations provide the context within which NSPCC services are delivered.

The first edition of this book has reached a wide audience and has been quoted in The Children Act Report 2002 (DFES, 2003). This paperback edition is updated in the light of recent policy, research and practice developments in the field.

Professor Jane Tunstill
*Honorary Member of
the NSPCC Council*

FOREWORD

I am very pleased to have been invited to contribute a Foreword to this timely and informative book. It is so encouraging to read a well presented and soundly based text that identifies the needs of children within the context of their families. This approach is reflected in the title of the book and it permeates each chapter. The author tackles the key issues and in doing so addresses two of the matters which concern me most about current social care practice for children and families.

The first is the general failure to implement the Children Act 1989. On the very first page Ruth Gardner reminds us that the services are intended to: 'safeguard and promote the welfare of children within their area who are in need; and as far as is consistent with that duty, to promote the upbringing of such children by their families'. Alas, all too often service provision ignores this section and, instead, only begins at section 47. This preoccupation with a narrow definition of child protection deprives many children and families of the help they need. I wonder how many tragedies to children could have been prevented by earlier intervention and support. Services to children and families should not be so crisis driven. Those who work in support of children must develop the skills and the confidence to work with families.

Secondly, it is a matter of regret that even now so little social care provision is informed by research. There is no justification for social care not taking place within the discipline of an academic framework. The author sets out clearly a series of research findings that ought to provide indicators of those families who could benefit from help and support. In the aftermath of the Victoria Climbié Inquiry, the Green Paper 'Every Child Matters' and the new Children Bill, the time is opportune to transform the vision and practice of work with children and families.

Ruth Gardner's book strikes just the right notes to encourage us to respond to the challenge of change. I congratulate her and hope that her book will be widely read and used.

Lord Laming
September 2004

ACKNOWLEDGEMENTS

Thanks to all who helped and supported the research project. Thanks, firstly, to all the children and parents who agreed to be interviewed and who came to group meetings and workshops to talk about family support. Professor Jane Tunstill, Honorary Member of the NSPCC Council, gave invaluable advice and support throughout the project. Dr Ilan Katz, then Head of the Evaluation Department at NSPCC, ensured the smooth running of the research process. Dr Lorraine Wallis provided valuable expertise for the data analysis and figures. Joan Derbyshire formatted the manuscript for publication.

Initial discussions were held with a number of researchers in this field who gave helpful material and advice. They include Marion Brandon and Jo Connolly (UEA) and Nick Frost (Leeds). The NSPCC Library provided a great deal of help with background material.

Although the list below is not exhaustive, my particular thanks to Wendy Alexander, Sandeep Atkar, Ralph Bamber, Patricia Bamford, Amanda Bunn, Jacquelyn Burke, Lyn Carruthers, Bruce Clark, Chris Cloke, Richard Cotmore, Sue Crane, Alison Cummings, Carol Curtis, Jane Freeman, Rajinder Ghataora, Andy Gill, Susan Glover, Barry Graham, Gary Holmes, Sylvia Kerly, Jo Kimberlee, Caroline Leahy, Rod MacDonald, Liz Mackenzie, Laura MacFarlane, Jeff Mesie, Mary Mills, Patricia Moran, Ann Norburn, Phillip Noyes, Lucy Thorpe, Jim Waters, Karen Wright, Dot Yellen, and Paul Whalley.

The content of this book is the author's work and does not represent the views of any group or organisation.

REPORT OF THE COMMITTEE ON LOCAL AUTHORITY & ALLIED PERSONAL SOCIAL SERVICES 1968

Although we often do not know how to prevent social distress or where our efforts can best be concentrated, it is, we believe, right to strive toward prevention. We are convinced that the more integrated service we suggest, together with an increase in resources, will give an opportunity to think and plan and to undertake work other than that caused by families and individuals in the late or final steps of dependence, disintegration and despair ... In particular we need a better basis for reaching choices between alternatives when the decisions once made may be irreversible (like adoption) and have far-reaching consequences for human happiness.

CONCLUSION 115

We cannot emphasise too strongly the part which research must play in the creation and maintenance of an effective family service. Social planning is an illusion without adequate facts; and the adequacy of services mere speculation without evaluation. Nor is it sufficient for research to be done spasmodically, however good it be. It must be a continuing process, accepted as a familiar and permanent feature of any department or agency concerned with social provision.

PAUL BOATENG, MINISTER OF HEALTH, JULY 1997

One major thrust of this government is to recognise that early interventions are not only the most effective in terms of enhancing people's lives and opportunities but also the most cost effective. It is for example better to use resources on early intervention and outreach work in high risk communities than putting a young person through the criminal justice system . . . this goes back to having a vision for children's services that embraces all children in terms of their own particular needs. There is, therefore, to be much closer liaison between the various departmental responsibilities—health, social services, education, employment, juvenile justice, and social security—in order to develop a coherent set of children's policies.

THE VICTORIA CLIMBIÉ INQUIRY 2003 (PARA. 1.30)

It is not possible to separate the protection of children from wider support to families. Indeed, often the best protection for a child is achieved by the timely intervention of family support services.

1

INTRODUCTION AND SUMMARY OF FINDINGS

This book gives an account of work undertaken with parents and children by the project staff of the National Society for the Prevention of Cruelty to Children (NSPCC). It describes the family support they offer, which we investigated and reported between 1998 and 2001. A second phase of the study, 2002 to 2004, has just ended and this updated edition gives an update on the most recent findings. Why is this work important? and How was it investigated? are some of the issues that this book deals with.

The NSPCC is a national charity offering services from over a hundred and fifty projects across England, Northern Ireland and Wales. Its first aim, according to its Charter, is 'to prevent the public and the private wrongs of children'. The Society pioneered child protection legislation and systems in this country and is today one of the most influential voices in our current debate about their effectiveness. Although many identify it with child rescue, the NSPCC was unusual among the large nineteenth century charities in working with families in their own homes, in using its legal powers to keep them together wherever possible, and in not setting up child care institutions (Malton, 2000).

Its inspectors began to recognise the complexity of the 'evil' of child abuse, including contributory factors such as domestic violence, poverty, ill health and isolation. Their accounts showed that with some assistance most parents could recover from a crisis to 'normal' functioning and could keep their children safe. Their efforts and observations contributed to the foundation of social work. The NSPCC can thus claim to have been one of the earliest testing grounds for family-based preventative action and support.

The projects we looked at for this study were offering services they identified as consistent with S.17 Part III of the Children Act 1989, services intended

to safeguard and promote the welfare of children within their area who are in need; and as far as is consistent with that duty, to promote the upbringing of such children by their families. (The Children Act, 1989)

They thus provide a sample of activities, usually funded in partnership with local authorities, intended to *prevent* (by early intervention) children coming to harm or unnecessarily having to be accommodated away from home, and to *promote* the strengths and aspirations of family members.

These two elements, *prevention* of damage and *promotion* of strengths, feature in more or less equal balance in most definitions of what 'family support' is intended to achieve. Some definitions centre on the activity itself, and are descriptive:

> any activity or facility provided either by statutory agencies or by community groups or individuals, aimed at providing advice and support to parents to help them in bringing up their children. (Audit Commission, 1994)

Other definitions emphasise the ethos of family support, i.e. working with the family's own strengths and in its immediate context—an important theme in this book:

> promoting competence and meeting basic developmental needs of children and families in 'normalised' settings; by teaching practical life skills and by providing environmental supports, as opposed to uncovering and treating underlying pathology. (Whittaker, 1991)

More specifically, according to Warren,

> family support practice means providing social support networks for children and their families within a range of formal and informal organisations, thus avoiding social exclusion. (Warren, 1997)

This definition is a good summary of what the NSPCC's family support projects say that they are doing. But additionally, when an 'underlying pathology' becomes apparent, staff and volunteers have necessary preparation and training to take this on. They are able to offer more intensive help such as one-to-one counselling, or can support a child or an adult to seek help. The NSPCC's projects thus fall within another definition of family support:

> a way of dealing with life crisis and problems, including abuse within families, which takes account of any strengths and positive relationships within those same families which could assist recovery. Formal interventions are minimised and, where necessary, are introduced in a timely, sensitive way with as little damage to the family as possible. (Gardner, 1998)

Working with family violence and harm to children is a high risk area, where mistakes can be serious if not fatal. This study seeks evidence to develop our understanding of early preventative intervention that is capable of protecting children, while remaining accessible to families. The resources are simply not available, even if it were desirable, to apply child protection procedures to investigate every apprehended risk to a child. The referral and assessment processes filter out the majority of reported cases of possible risk to children, without their receiving either child protection or family support (Department of Health, 1995). Many cases of risk are not brought to statutory agencies at all:

> the problem confronting child protection professionals is both over-reporting and under-reporting; over-reporting of signs, risks and fears, and under-reporting of actual harm and injury. (Wattam, 1997)

This book gives the results of an examination of the NSPCC's family support over a two-year period, commissioned by the charity from Royal Holloway College, University of London. The remainder of the introduction briefly describes the aims of the research and the methods used. Details of the methodology are given in the relevant chapter and the appendices, for readers with a research interest. We summarise the key findings and their immediate implications for policy and practice. Other recent research findings on family support are also set out. An overview of family support, with a broad range of recommendations, is provided in the final chapter.

The original aims of the research were:

- to identify NSPCC services and activities that can be shown to support families (children, parents or carers) effectively within their communities
- to ascertain the extent to which NSPCC services are valued by key stakeholders as delivering a family support service.

By 'effective' and 'valued' we mean being able to offer robust evidence that the services achieve their stated aims in supporting children and families, in ways that conform to or exceed acknowledged practice standards, and at optimal cost.

Relevant objectives or sub-tasks included:

- identifying those interested in the NSPCC's family support, i.e. the key stakeholders, and obtaining their views
- identifying the range of support services and activities and their intended outcomes
- identifying measures of effectiveness, relating outputs to outcomes, and of efficiency, relating outputs to inputs
- describing activities that, either singly or in conjunction with other supports, formal or informal, appear to achieve identified outcomes.

Pecora *et al.* (1995) have identified four types of evaluation questions for family support services, and have suggested appropriate methodologies for addressing them. They are:

- questions about *family support needs*, which can be answered by survey methods;
- questions about the *type and process of service delivery*, best answered via case records and other data;
- questions about *outcome*, which can be answered by experimental or quasi-experimental studies or by management information data, depending on the size of population; and
- questions about *cost assessment*, relying on financial data.

A mix of quantitative and qualitative, more descriptive approaches can be used to address all four types of research questions, and this study has used such a mix, in order to examine each 'layer' of family support—children, their families and the projects within their communities. Well aware of concerns about the quality of research evidence for the effectiveness of services, we do not claim to have proof of family support producing the changes we describe over a six-month period. The changes themselves, however, are evidenced in the words of those directly involved: children, parents, staff of the NSPCC and other agencies working with families, as well as by analysis of questionnaire scores before and after six months of family support intervention, where (with family members' consent) we use tested research schedules.

Tested questionnaires were used to assess child behavioural problems and parental stress, vulnerability and ill health, scoring a series of answers on these subjects and comparing responses six months later. We were particularly interested in families' personal networks of support and use of resources in their neighbourhood. We devised a questionnaire to assess these perceptions, again over a six-month period. These are tentative findings, but they are, we believe, some of the most interesting. These research tools were used consistently by the same researcher in six research projects across England, described in Chapter 8. Finally, using a survey for all the NSPCC's projects, we evaluated components of their family support, in order to ensure that the research sites were reasonably representative, and to see the wider picture of provision.

CHILDREN'S BEHAVIOUR

Key Findings

- When we asked what they wanted of family support, most parents sought help in relation to children's behaviour, particularly that of school-age children. Where help is only available for pre-school children, parents were adapting the advice for use with their older children.
- Parents we interviewed wanted support (e.g. practical assistance such as day care, advice or other help) for half of the children in their families.

Parents saw most (69%) of these children as having positive, or pro-social, characteristics but saw a higher proportion (71%) as having behavioural difficulties. Again, most of these difficulties were 'severe'.

- There was a cluster of problems around hyperactivity and conduct, and another around emotional and peer relationships. Bullying and being bullied featured highly.
- The degree of difficulty (as assessed by parents) grew with age. Nine was the average age (for both boys and girls) at which children's difficulties were seen as presenting obvious problems and stress to the family and others.
- Most problems with children under three had been resolved within six months, and there was also a significant improvement in the behaviour of children over three whom we followed up, although we cannot specify cause and effect.
- Parents identified children's behaviour as a major source of stress in the family, increasing their own sense of inadequacy. They often linked severe behavioural problems in children, to family violence and the child's having suffered emotional and/or other harm.
- Children, parents and other agencies frequently attributed improvements (at least in part) to the same aspects of family support activity. These were
  - direct work with children, helping them to improve their social skills and express their wishes and feelings successfully, both within and outside the family (see Chapter 4);
  - work with parents to identify specific behavioural problems and ways of handling them constructively (see Chapter 4); and
  - assistance with speedy referrals for specialist help or other advocacy, for example, about behaviour in school or possible exclusion. Projects also offered direct access to the NSPCC's services for dealing with children's or parents' experiences of conflict, assault or abuse (see Chapter 8).
- Where parents' existing informal network of friends and family was strong, children achieved or maintained 'positive' behaviour scores over six months. Parents with good informal support also had more positive health and stress scores after six months (see Chapter 6).

Implications for Policy and Practice

- Helplines offer one accessible source of advice, but parents need face-to-face support (e.g. counselling and groupwork) to be much more widespread and easy to obtain. Contact with other parents, normalising the most common difficulties and reducing isolation, needs to be made easier.
- Expertise in child psychology and psychiatry is seen as remote, and restricted by administrative procedures. These skills need to be more readily available to all family support services so as to identify and seek

prompt and suitable support for children with more serious difficulties. This could be in the form of sessions with family support workers in schools or other community bases, and/or joint groupwork.

- The most distressed children were exhibiting harmful and self-harming behaviour. Many had not been referred for specialist help, or appointments had not been kept, or parents described what they saw as being blamed for their child's problems. In some areas there were complaints from parents, family support staff and teachers about the inaccessibility of, and lack of partnership with, child mental health services. This study suggests that the variability of child mental health services (Social Services Inspectorate, 1999; Health Advisory Service, 1995) has not markedly improved and continues to pose major problems for families and mainstream services, despite the government's efforts to stimulate new thinking (see p. 44).

COMPONENTS OF PARENTAL STRESS

Key Findings

- Nearly half of the parents and carers suffered serious health and stress problems at the first interview. These findings are consistent with other recent studies of family support in Britain (see p. 39). Many of these adults had not been referred for specialist help, or had received what they perceived as a poor response from the health service.
- After six months, the majority of parents we followed up summarised their health as 'about the same'. Questionnaire scores indicated that they were optimistic, since nearly half had deteriorated in some aspect of their physical or mental health.
- Lower levels of parental stress and ill health at the second interview were significantly associated with parents' assessment of children's behavioural difficulty as having improved to, or maintained at, a level of concern below the threshold score (i.e. the score indicating difficulties that may require specialist help).
- A higher proportion of parents who had received a structured service, such as one-to-one counselling, volunteer visiting or parent's groups, had maintained or achieved levels of ill health and stress below the threshold score, compared to parents who had received occasional support. The type and size of the sample means that this finding is not conclusive, but merits further investigation.
- A higher level of vulnerability in terms of past life experiences (e.g. early parenthood, multiple moves, violence) was associated with:
  - greater health and/or stress problems (first interview)
  - greater behavioural difficulties in a child (first interview) and behaviour

maintaining or reaching a level of concern above the threshold score (second interview)
- lower levels of informal (friends and family) support.
- About a third of the parents interviewed had at some stage sought assistance from the family support project to discuss and deal with their own past experiences of being harmed as children, and/or later experiences of violence. Resolving these experiences was often, in their view, crucial to their own mental health and parenting capacity.
- The small number of fathers and other male carers we interviewed had health and vulnerability scores, and needs for support, similar to those of women.

Implications for Policy and Practice

- Needs related to parental health and stress appear to be relatively neglected in the development of family support, a finding that has not changed from a previous study of local authority preventative social work. Hitherto, family support providers have not *systematically* assessed, or sought to address, the physical and mental health of parents unless these obviously impinge on their parenting capacity, and sometimes not even then (Gardner, 1991).
- Family support services should have formal links to primary health care, including but not confined to health visiting, and their evaluation should be linked *both* to health service targets for adults *and* to developmental targets for children in need. This study endorses the British Medical Association's (BMA) recommendations on health visiting: 'health authorities should initiate health visitor led identification of post-natal depression, and specific training should be offered' (BMA, 1999).
- Where parents agree, their vulnerability in terms of past experience should be assessed with the parent her/himself, and ways of addressing continuing difficulties suggested. Parents may not want or need help immediately, but there is strong evidence from this study that many take up specialised help, for example therapy, but only by choice if and when they have gained trust and confidence to do so. They see this help as crucial to improvements for both themselves and their children. Therapy should be independent of any statutory involvement with the family.

NETWORKS OF SUPPORT

Key Findings

We asked parents about networks of support at three levels—informal (family and friends), semi-informal (the community, including the project) and formal (professional networks, such as health and social services).

It must be emphasised that the questionnaire devised for this aspect of the research is not fully tested and these are tentative findings.

- Parents found most support from friends and family (in that order) and one of their main aims in using the project was to create or to enlarge their informal network of support.
- Parents' perception of their level of informal support was negatively associated with their scores for vulnerability, stress and ill health and their assessment of children's behavioural difficulty. In other words, the greater their informal support network, the lower the degree of difficulty parents perceived in these areas, and vice versa, the weaker their informal support network, the greater the degree of difficulty. Parents with greater informal support at first interview tended to assess children's behaviour as having maintained or attained a level below the threshold for high concern after six months. This perception of lower 'worry' levels at second interview was related to a more positive perception of the neighbourhood and perceived support from all sources, which we sum up as the 'community climate'.
- Outside of friends and family, the local NSPCC project was the source of greatest support and the single most often mentioned source of support. For half the parents, the project was their only link with the wider community. It was especially important for the 10% of parents who could name no family and friends from whom they obtained support.
- Family members, NSPCC and other agency staff made links between informal, community and professional support. For instance, the majority of parents came to the family support project on a friend's recommendation or by informal contact with the project's staff or users. Through the project, many had obtained confidence and active support to use local resources, including professional help. Some had become helpers themselves, and some had gained qualifications. On the other hand, professionals said they gained a wider repertoire of preventive options and received more appropriate referrals if they had good links with one another and with community groups. In other words, we believe that there is an important transfer of skills and knowledge between levels of the support network, which potentially improves the 'community climate', the safety and the supportiveness of the community, for children.

Phase Two of the Research: Early Findings

While this study went to press a second phase of the research had started and this section brings the reader up to date with the most recent findings.

Our aim in this phase has been to find out more about current demand for NSPCC family support. A group of 18 projects monitored every contact by or on behalf of service-users over a five-day period including visits, phone-calls, letters and e-mails. We have also undertaken a further 100 in-depth interviews with parents, following up as many as possible after six to nine months as in Phase One. We therefore have evidence on family support from two national surveys and nearly 200 interviews. The interviews have used a similar format in Phase Two but with additional questionnaires on material resources (Gordon *et al.*, 2000); relationships (Gilgun, 1996); attachment style (Bifulco *et al.*, 2003); and parental discipline (Cawson *et al.*, 2000).

Demand for Family Support

The findings for a sub-group of projects indicate that NSPCC's family support provision attracts some 2600 contacts over a five-day period, relating to 1225 families with some 2000 children. Over 80% of the contacts were in person, giving a picture of high demand and physical access to the projects. Predictably, parents, mostly mothers, made over half (53%) of the week's contacts; children made a further third (29%) and professionals over a tenth (13%), suggesting that children make good use of the projects.

Needs and Concerns

The broad picture of needs presented to the projects includes adult relationship difficulties (26% of mentions); adult health or stress (15%); practical difficulties (e.g. childcare) (12%) and problems with parenting (12 %). Concerns about children were age-related with an apparent 'peak' of concerns (41%) about boys at age 9–12. Concerns about girls were more evenly distributed across the age bands with a higher proportion (26%) at ages 3–4. Teenagers of both sexes were the next largest proportions.

The overlap between family support and child protection noted throughout Phase One is seen again in the finding that approximately one-sixth of families had been referred to social services at some stage, many had experienced one or more assessments and just under a tenth of families had had one or more children on a child protection register. In over half these cases neglect was the main cause for concern, with other actual or possible harm mentioned in a further third.

While the survey was necessarily a broad-brush approach, it gives a useful impression of the range of problems addressed by family support services as a whole, as a backdrop to individual interviews (Bunn and Gardner, forthcoming).

Early Findings from Phase Two: Interviews with Parents

Over a third (35%) of parents had high scores for health and stress problems and these were associated with being a single parent; having concerns about or difficulties with a child; having difficult family relationships; and feeling insecure in relation to attachment. There is an indication that parents' use or approval of punitive methods of discipline with children may relate to difficulty or insecurity in key relationships, but this needs further investigation.

Parents had concerns about over a third (38%) of their children (N = 253) and of these approximately half (56%) had high scores on the Strengths and Difficulties questionnaire. Children about whom there were concerns were more likely to be boys, to have high scores for emotional and conduct difficulties and to have lower 'pro-social' scores, as well as more likely to be receiving an NSPCC service.

To summarise, the most recent findings offer a profile of families and concerns that is consistent with the completed study reported here, and open a window on other issues.

Implications for Policy and Practice

- These findings need to be explored further and tested in a larger study of more rigorous design.
- They reinforce research and evaluation that suggest links between family stress and the immediate environment, both in the UK (Gibbons and Wilkinson, 1990; Holman, 1988; Warren, 1997) and in American research over three decades (Furstenburg, 1999; Maluccio, 1998).
- The role of family support in promoting informal networks, and the protective effect of these networks in relation to family stress and child safety, should be further explored.
- Activities designed to strengthen networks of family and friends should receive particular attention in terms of evaluated developments, for instance, the use of volunteer visitors and other befriending schemes for both children and parents; the extended use of groupwork and other types of support networks, especially with men, some of whom feel even more isolated from support than do women; support for children in maintaining contact with a separated parent (lack of contact and conflicted contact were major sources of reported depression and anxiety for children); advice and advocacy in approaching and negotiating with professionals, for instance with teachers, or in helping families to keep children safe through child protection investigations.

OTHER POLICY AND PRACTICE ISSUES RAISED
BY THE RESEARCH

- Child Adolescent Mental Health Services (CAMHS) should offer more direct support to families and front-line staff (as recommended by the Audit Commission, 1994; BMA, 1999) and be managed at the highest level to evidence achievement of this role and of specific preventative targets. Current experiments with multi-disciplinary child behaviour support teams including CAMHS staff should be closely monitored and their results reported as widely as possible.

- Some NSPCC projects offered family support services in the community, as well as direct access to more specialised services such as therapy groups, one-to-one counselling, video-home guidance and other behaviour management techniques. In these circumstances, family members (children or parents) could usually receive intensive help from a known source once they had the confidence to refer themselves. Even where referral had to be made to the local authority's child protection service, some projects had the skills to assess and manage risk in partnership with that service and to limit the trauma of the investigation process. In addition, once the crisis was resolved, the family was already receiving a local service and just as they obtained more intensive help, could reduce it over time. This 'maintenance support', sometimes minimal but extended over months or years, was seen as crucial by many parents who had suffered crises. It could ensure direct contact with, and a known source of help for, the children once statutory monitoring had ceased.

- This closer integration of a child safety approach with family support is not confined to the NSPCC, but the organisation has a long history of applying it. The NSPCC has developed explicit ground rules and standards, rather than lengthy procedures, which appear to have the confidence of the majority of service users and partner agencies. Having specified the framework, skills and knowledge base (discussed in Chapter 7) in greater detail, the NSPCC should promote this model of family support.

- In addition to the approach described above, many of the NSPCC's family support projects undertook evaluation of the satisfaction levels of those who had used the service. An interest in evaluation and openness to criticism was the norm; there seemed a real possibility of reflective practice. This is in stark contrast to the current situation in some local authority children's departments, where staffing levels and morale are a cause of grave concern. As part of the 'challenge' and 'compare' stages of Best Value reviews, greater exchange of front-line staff, working methods and learning opportunities between organisations should be encouraged to allow for fresh thinking and practice development.

SUMMARIES OF RELEVANT RESEARCH

The final part of this introductory chapter provides the research context for this study by summarising relevant research on family support. The studies illustrate Pecora's typology of evaluation methodologies in family support (see pp. 3–4).

Gibbons and Wilkinson (1990) considered the first two types of research questions outlined earlier, that is, *family support needs* and *type and process of service* delivery, with some hypotheses about short-term outcomes.

Methodology: They studied families referred to social services departments in two areas. In one of the areas, voluntary organisations had set up local family support projects. Two referred groups, 144 families in all, were compared with 359 families drawn from one of the localities, partly through random sampling and partly through selection of addresses adjacent to the random sample.

The main carers in these families were interviewed using a range of measures and indicators of income, housing, health, family problems, etc. A total of 122 parents were re-interviewed after four months. Qualitative measures, such as degree of satisfaction with support, were included.

Findings: Some of the findings, which refer to family support practice in the 1980s, were as follows:

- Differences in family composition and material needs were striking as between referred and non-referred families. The former had far more lone (divorced) parents and material disadvantage.
- Parents in referred families were also more isolated and less supported, as well as experiencing more family conflict than did non-referred families.
- Social workers were often dealing with financial difficulties and child abuse referrals and not generally looking for underlying emotional problems. 'Duty social workers did not carry out the kinds of assessment that would have revealed other difficulties'.
- Social services in one area had supported voluntary organisations as providers, but the new services had not affected social work practice; social services managers and practitioners would need to be freed for developmental work.
- User groups were not diverse or representative of local communities; they were mostly white women and their children.
- Projects had more similarities than differences, but tended to be either service-oriented *or* community development oriented.
- Local family support projects could provide more choice, flexibility and participation than could statutory services, as well as indicate areas for service improvement.

- They successfully attracted families under stress, but this might serve to stigmatise them for some local people.
- Other forms of provision, such as playgroups, differentially attracted advantaged families.
- Partnership between the statutory and voluntary sector was difficult to maintain over time as priorities changed, yet funding organisations were not always prepared to hand projects over to local management groups to ensure survival.

Outcomes:

- Families in an area with voluntary projects reported more contact with a variety of family support resources. This, and especially the use of day care of various kinds, was associated with improvement in family problems.
- The research suggested that a network of family support in communities does indeed assist parents under stress in overcoming family problems.
- The effectiveness and cost of different kinds of provision need to be tested and evaluated against their stated objectives.

Frost *et al.* (1996) studied the effectiveness of a voluntary home-visiting scheme—Homestart—intended to provide regular support, friendship and practical support to young families (predominantly mothers) under stress in their own homes so as to prevent family crisis and breakdown.
   Methodology: This included survey data on 307 families and interviews with service users, volunteers and referrers concerning 46 families. Groups made up of these partners to the work generated the desired outcomes for the services, used as the basis for questions about effectiveness.
   Outcomes:

- The majority of women (51%) saw an improvement in emotional well being and thought that their informal network had been extended over the six months of the study.
- A similar percentage saw a shift for the better in parenting difficulties.
- Substantial minorities reported improvements in the relationship with partners (42%) or with professionals (37%). There was an overlap between these groups.

Aldgate and Bradley (1999) studied short-term fostering as a means of family support. All families who were offered short-term fostering in four local authorities were approached, until 60 cases had been recruited.
   Methodology: Interviews were conducted with children, parents, social workers and carers. The first three groups were interviewed when accommodation for the child had been agreed, and again once the arrangement had

ended or after nine months, whichever came first. A standardised test was used with parents and children, in addition to information from the social worker's assessment. Overall aims were to study the nature and process of the service and discover whether the family had remained intact; whether their problems had lessened; whether social work aims had been met; and whether users thought that the service had met their needs.

Outcomes:

- Over the period of the study, the standardised test indicated that more parents felt in control.
- They thought that the service had allowed them to tackle major problems, they had improved their social support systems and they were seen to be managing their relationships with children and partners in a more constructive way.
- Comparing themselves to foster carers looking after their children, they had become aware of their disadvantages in terms of income and accommodation.
- Overall they found the service 'a resounding success'.
- Most children thought that they, and/or their parents, had benefited, but the process had been isolating and anxiety-provoking for some.

In terms of the aim to test short-term accommodation as preventing family breakdown, one would need a longer follow-up and also an equivalent group who had received routine, or no support. The researchers conclude that 'the needs of children in this study had been assessed as sufficiently serious to access priority services—(they) would have been struggling without services. Some families would have benefited from the availability of support such as drop-in family centres or befriending schemes. (These) might have prevented the deterioration of some families to the point where early risk had brought them to seek help from social workers... short-term accommodation, therefore, needs to be available as one of a broad range of services for families under stress'.

Thoburn *et al.* (2000) studied family support in cases of emotional maltreatment and neglect.

Methodology: A sample of cases was selected from all referrals over a given period to three social services areas. Of these, the majority had been referred because of concern about neglect or emotional maltreatment. A smaller sample of families in need requesting a service without these concerns was used for comparison purposes. A total of 122 families were interviewed, and 108 were re-interviewed between 12 and 18 months later, about the service they had sought, their local support systems, health and well being and children's behaviour; standardised tests were used. Social services and health records were available for most families.

Outcomes:

- On follow-up, the level of stress had improved for just over half the families.
- In nearly half, the health and development of the children had also improved or not deteriorated.
- In 72% of cases no further referral was made regarding maltreatment or neglect.
- Stress levels had increased in *more* of the families requesting a 'specific service' than in the families where neglect or emotional harm was an issue— possibly, the researchers suggest, because children in the first group more often had general health and development needs.
- There was no significant association between outcome and the level of support to the main carer at first interview, but the 'trend was for better outcomes for those with emotional and practical support'.

Overall, even in this reasonably large study, it was not possible to associate any one type of service with better or worse outcomes. Reviewing family factors, service factors and outcomes, 'the characteristics of the family appeared to have the greatest influence on outcome for parents and children'.

The researchers concluded that, for some families, repeated short periods of 'task-centred' help with new referrals and assessments may be counterproductive. More sustained intervention, evaluated over a longer period, will be needed, rather than a succession of short interventions.

> family centres, which can provide continuity . . . even when key workers move on, provide a particularly appropriate service setting. The intensity of services provided to each family will rise and fall in response to the stresses on family members.

Like Aldgate and Bradley's study, this tells us about needs and processes in family support, as well as the difficulty of attributing outcomes to specific services even over the medium term with a fairly large sample.

A recent study by Tunstill and Aldgate (2000) set out 'to monitor and evaluate the provision and to some extent the delivery of family support services to a group of children in need, and to their immediate and extended families'.

Methodology: The study focused on families with children in the middle age group, across seven local authority areas, excluding child protection cases and referrals of children with disabilities. A total of 93 parents and 41 children were interviewed after referral, and again six months later. Family problems and stresses, expectations of Social Services and other agencies and the effect of the help offered were subjects covered in the parent interviews, with children being asked a similar range of questions.

Findings:

- Data on children in need 'were often so scattered, so varied in terms of sample size and so uncollated, that they could not serve to provide a comprehensive picture'.
- In this respect, little had changed since a review of implementation of The Children Act 1989 (Tunstill and McBeath, 1995).
- Children in middle childhood aged 7–12 years, received few family support services.
- There appeared to be very uneven and, in some authorities, inadequate overall development of services for children in need.
- Parents hoped for a range of benefits from family support services, advocacy, help with child development and improvement in family problems and relationships, including with children and partners.
- Just under 40% of children hoped that parental conflict would be resolved.
- Professionally referred families were less likely to be turned away, and also received more services over longer periods.
- Cases of social deprivation were least likely, and cases of ill health most likely, to receive a family support service.

Outcomes:

- Benefits exceeded parents' expectations in cases of parental ill health; practical problems were alleviated more frequently than anticipated; and relief of stress and child development difficulties occurred in most cases.
- Improvement in family relationships occurred in 41% of cases where it had been anticipated.
- The majority of parents found social services helpful and more than half, though happy overall with the services received, wanted more (i.e. they were unsatisfied rather than dissatisfied).

Tunstill and Aldgate conclude that, given the increasing pressure to raise thresholds and exclude referrals, information to families about, and access to, all available services must be improved. They argue, as does Thoburn's study, that parents need to be able to opt in and out of family support over time.

More recent studies have extended our knowledge of family support, in terms of:

- studies of specific family circumstances and events, e.g. separation
- training for parents and parenting programmes
- parents' role in pupil achievement and adjustment
- specific types of family support, e.g. family centres
- support for specific groups, e.g. black and ethnic minority families, families with a disabled child, families with a child with behavioural problems or combinations of these issues
- early results from national evaluations of central government initiatives in this field.

An example from each of these areas is given below with a selection of findings relevant to this study. The chapter concludes by drawing out common themes and messages.

Studies of Specific Family Circumstances and Events

Quinton (2004) summarised 14 studies sponsored by the Department of Health in the 'Supporting Parents Research Initiative', carried out in the decade from 1994. The study reported in this book was undertaken with a similar perspective,

> to broaden research in children's social care to consider how all parents might be helped to look after their children well and to move away from an emphasis on more marked family and parenting problems. One idea was that there might be many family and community supports that could be 'mobilized' to this end. (Quinton, 2004).

Of the 14 studies, one of relevance in this context concerned parenting in poor environments (Ghate and Hazel, 2002). The study was designed to discover what parents living in materially disadvantaged communities want from social support and how better support for parents can be achieved.

Methodology: A representative national interview survey of 1754 parents, randomly selected from the top 30 per cent of disadvantaged areas. The Poor Parenting Environments (PPE) Index was developed for the study. There was a qualitative follow-up study of 40 parents in especially disadvantaged circumstances.

Findings: Key findings in this study include:

- Parents living in poor environments were in considerably worse physical and mental health than other adults of the same age in the general population.

- Parents' physical and mental health problems were highly interrelated, and were also likely to go along with poor child physical health and having a behaviourally or emotionally 'difficult' child.
- Lone parents were much less likely than parents with partners to say they were 'coping' with parenting. However, parents who had an 'unsupportive' partner had the same (low) rate of coping as lone parents.

Five key factors predicted problems in 'coping with parenting', once poverty was controlled for:

- being a lone parent, and/or having
- a difficult child
- poor mental health
- a complex of family and household problems
- a large family.

What parents wanted from semi-formal and formal services were:

- increased accessibility (e.g. longer opening hours)
- expansion of facilities in existing services (e.g. more staff on duty)
- improvements in staff quality and training
- a wider profile of users, and
- written information for parents.

A second very relevant study summarised by Quinton, of family centres (Tunstill, Hughes and Aldgate, forthcoming), was intended to:

- examine the potential of family centres as a gateway to family support services
- explore the extent to which family centres facilitate or develop links with informal support networks within the community, and
- explore the potential for family centres to act as coordinators of family support.

Methodology: This included a postal survey of over 400 Centres in England; interviews with over 100 service users, centre managers, and other professionals.
Findings: Family centres:

- provide access to a wide range of services via joint work and networking
- have a key role in development of parenting skills from informal to intensive help
- could provide specialist help without undue stigma or delay

- have adapted to changing needs and demands by developing existing resources including staff skills.

The difficulties faced by the centres include restructuring and redeployment of staff to other priorities, pressure away from open access towards increased specialisation, and short-term or restricted funding. However, overall the centres were seen to be well placed to provide community-based services for children and families (and to) have the capacity to meet the needs of children and parents without sacrificing one to the other (Quinton, 2004).

Training for Parents: Parenting Programmes

Barrett (2003) gives an overview of a selection of parenting programmes for families who are struggling with specific issues or risks. She also summarises systematic reviews, meta-analysis and surveys of parenting programmes with associated information (websites, evaluation measures).

> The intention is to bring together in one volume key information, to a sufficient degree of sophistication, which generally helps funders and managers to make informed choices in an expanding and increasingly significant area of social intervention. (Barrett, 2003)

Findings:

- In order to be effective, interventions at a later stage of prevention need to be even more multi-focussed, flexible, adaptable and non-stigmatising than their earlier counterparts.
- Work is required to identify and classify discrete programme elements more systematically, so that their effectiveness can be better monitored.
- Programmes with a broader remit, influencing and engaging parents and children at home, in school and in the wider community, have the largest and longest-lasting effects.
- To be effective, parenting programmes need to ensure that they do not stigmatise or create dependency, and last long enough for change to be sustained.
- There is a particular need for more information about the needs of minority ethnic parents, including refugee families, e.g. how well the needs of these families are currently being met, and what else is needed.
- There is a need for new systems for exchange of information to be developed so that the skills, expertise and knowledge already available in many local areas can be recognised, effectively met and built upon.

Parents' Role in Pupil Achievement and Adjustment

A review of English language literature was conducted

> to establish research findings on the relationship between parental involvement, parental support and family education on pupil achievement and adjustment in schools. (Desforges and Abouchaar, 2003)

The central importance of this issue to current social policy is that it potentially links the support available to families with the support parents give their children's learning at home, and how children make use of this educationally. The review's recommendations are consistent with other findings, including those of this study.

Methodology: The review investigated the impact on pupil achievement and engagement of various factors:

- Support to parents, e.g. the provision of parenting skills training, advice, guidance for parents.
- Family learning, e.g. as parent-governor, reading to children, encouragement and help with homework.
- Parents' level of education.

Findings:

- Parental involvement takes many forms, including good parenting in the home (e.g. the provision of a secure and stable environment, intellectual stimulation, parent–child discussion, good models of constructive social and educational values and high aspirations relating to personal fulfilment and good citizenship); contact with school to share information; participation in school events; and participation in school governance.
- The extent and form of parental involvement is strongly influenced by family social class, maternal level of education, material deprivation, maternal psychosocial health and single parent status and, to a lesser degree, by family ethnicity.
- The extent of parental involvement diminishes as the child gets older and is strongly influenced at all ages by the child characteristically taking a very active mediating role.
- Parental involvement is strongly, positively influenced by the child's level of attainment: the higher the level of attainment, the more parents get involved.
- The most important finding from the point of view of this review is that parental involvement in the form of 'at-home good parenting' has a significant positive effect on the children's achievement and adjustment, even after all other factors shaping attainment have been taken out of the

equation. In the primary age range, the impact caused by different levels of parental involvement is much bigger than differences associated with variations in the quality of schools. The scale of the impact is evident across all social classes and all ethnic groups.

- For parental involvement to work, a whole community strategic approach is needed.

Studies of Specific Groups

Butt and Box (1998) examined the use of family centres by black and minority ethnic communities, considering whether family support services have been accessible to black children and their families and whether they have been valued by users and seen as effective. The relevance of the study is in the consistency of findings of patchy development of family support for black and ethnic minorities. There is some exciting innovation but, overall, a lack of strategy, funding and transfer of learning. The findings are particularly important given government's recent commitment to develop local children's centres (see p. 167).

Methodology: A questionnaire-based survey of 84 family centres in nine local authority areas in the UK plus interviews with staff and services users.

Findings:

- While equal opportunities policies were common, there was little evidence that the expansion of family centres included the aim to provide more services specifically to black families, or of funds to support development of services to these families. Ethnic monitoring systems for use of services existed in 55 of the 84 centres.
- Members of black and ethnic minority groups made most use of services targeted to them.
- For example, 23 centres provided specific services including English language support, and groups for women and for children. Beyond this they tended to use general services for children with or without adults; there was less use of services for adults, including parent programmes.
- An important factor is the presence of black workers; where there are more black workers there are more black service users.
- Black respondents were particularly likely to mention the benefits for children, in particular good quality day care; also, socialising opportunities and health and educational support.
- Many respondents commented on the way relationships had improved within their family as a result of the interventions.
- In most family centres men continue to play a limited role.
- Many family centres were in buildings without access or facilities for people with disabilities.

Early Findings from National Evaluations of Central Government Initiatives to Support Children and Families

Three such programmes are summarised here together, with some early findings from large-scale evaluations.

Sure Start (www.surestart.gov.uk)

This government programme aims to achieve better outcomes for children, parents and communities by:

- increasing the availability of good quality child care for all children;
- improving health, education and emotional development for young children under the age of four; and
- supporting parents as parents and in their aspirations towards employment.

This is to be achieved by:

- helping service development in disadvantaged areas alongside financial help of parents to afford child care;
- rolling out the principles driving the Sure Start approach to all services for children and parents.

Methodology: The National Evaluation of Sure Start (NESS) is in its first phase 2001–2008 and will assess the impact, implementation and cost-effectiveness of the programme. The implementation study has used three elements: an annual survey of all (260) Sure Start programme managers in the first four phases of development; 26 in-depth case studies and a series of themed evaluations.

Findings:

- The level of parental involvement was generally high and included fathers as well as (predominately) mothers.
- The voluntary sector was well represented in managing programmes, as were the main statutory agencies, with health being most common.
- Developing collaborative working relationships proved challenging, but there were good examples of multidisciplinary work, particularly in outreach and home visiting.
- Most programmes make good use of volunteers.

Ethnic monitoring of service users and staff also proved challenging, though most programmes make special provision for a range of groups including minority ethnic groups, young parents, refugees and asylum seekers (see Tunstill *et al.*, 2002).

The Children's Fund
(see www.cypu.gov.uk/corporate/childrensfund/index.cfm)

This programme targets disadvantaged children and young people aged 5–13 years old who are at risk of social exclusion. The programme aims to:

- help develop coherent preventive strategies for this group;
- support services in identifying children showing early signs of difficulty;
- provide and direct support to children and families;
- build capacity in the community by joint working; and
- actively involve children and their parent in planning and delivering services.

Methodology: The National Evaluation of the Children's Fund (NECF) has delivered a first annual report (NECF, 2003) based on evidence including interviews with all programme managers mapping local provision for this age group, and analysis of partnership plans.

Findings:

- Partnership working between statutory agencies, large voluntary organisations and to a lesser extent, smaller community groups was a distinctive and thriving feature of Children's Fund programme.
- There was a tension between local development and central (government) direction of the programme, for example an expectation from the centre that 25 per cent of funding would be allocated to crime prevention.
- Local partnerships were working to achieve participation by children and families but it was a slow and careful process.
- The majority of partnerships were aiming services at black and ethnic and other minority groups, whose take-up of Children's Fund services remained constant at around 30 per cent.
- In one year 2002–2003, the uptake of relevant support services by children and parents/carers had increased from 16,000 to 223,000.
- Partnerships believed that they were influencing local agencies in their development of a preventive strategy.

Extended Schools

Extended schools are ones that provide a range of services and activities often beyond the school day to help meet the needs of pupils, their families and the wider community. There is no blueprint for activities but they could include child care, adult learning, health and community facilities. The Education Act (2002) enables schools to directly provide such services and 25 local education authorities have received up to £2000 each to act as pathfinders in 2002–2003.

Methodology: A report of the evaluation of pathfinder projects (Cummings, Dyson and Todd, 2003) is based on visits to all the projects, analysis of documentary evidence, detailed case studies of ten projects and interviews with stakeholders including those using the services.

Findings:

- Extended schools have the potential to improve pupil attainment, attendance, motivation and behaviour.
- They can achieve greater parental involvement, e.g. through family literacy, information technology classes, helping parents to understand the children's school curriculum.
- Collaboration between agencies requires a careful and sustained process of trust-building where partners seek to understand each others aims, priorities and working methods. It is important that the process is given ample time and develops through a series of progressively more ambitious ventures (see above for reference).
- Genuine community consultation and participation are necessary but as these are difficult to achieve, many schools find it helpful to work with partners who are more experienced in this field.
- Viewing extended schools as time-limited and, additionally-funded 'projects' may become less effective over time. A different funding model may be needed as the extended activities become more (albeit to varying degrees) central to the role of the school.

SUMMARY

Over the period of this study, the focus for children and family services has shifted, from addressing individual need to achieving targets for whole populations, defined as disadvantaged in broadly economic terms, and also, in some cases, as at risk of social exclusion. This follows the policy-led provision funded by central government and monitored by the Department for Education and Science.

Research and evaluation approaches have modified accordingly. Compared to the earlier studies presented above, more recent work tends to articulate policy objectives in relation to the target population(s), then evaluates what has or has not been achieved. It less often describes specific services, individual experiences, or the detailed process of meeting need, perhaps with some loss of the diversity and depth of views that come through good qualitative studies. We gain the benefit of much larger data-sets and more quantitative analysis, a better understanding of the target populations, and an overview of service configurations. Certain interventions are seen to offer evidence of the type of outcomes being sought; for instance, in terms of children's attainment in school, these interventions include active parental support for learning in the home, and early nursery education. In general, community-based support programmes for parents – whether in family centres, Sure Start programmes or extended schools – appear to be popular with their target populations, but hard to grow where collaborative work is not already established. This is important because the evidence increasingly suggests that universal and targeted services work best interactively, and not in separate streams with discrete access points (see, for instance, Hall and Elliman, 2003). We still know too little about what is most useful for particular groups such as fathers, black and ethnic minority or disabled parents, and too little about the child's viewpoint; but these perspectives are at least attracting more attention and research funding (for instance the Children's Research Centre at the Open University; see Rix, 2004). Evidence of effectiveness will be crucial, but just as helpful will be transparency and learning at the early stages, rather than only when serious errors have been made, about what is not working. Willingness to learn from parents and children themselves would be especially valuable here; many parents we interviewed simply wanted their children to have a happy childhood, as the best preparation for a fulfilling and positive life, and asking children what would make them happy is a good way forward.

2

ABOUT THE FAMILIES

This chapter profiles the adults and children we interviewed at the six research projects. For the sake of anonymity, these projects have been named Metropolitan Suburb or Met S; Metropolitan Outskirts, Met O; New Estate, New E; Seaside, Sea S; Inner city, Inner C; and Garden City, Garden C. They are described in Chapter 8. The 88 parents and carers were aged from 18 to 63 years; some were looking after pre-school-age grandchildren (see Figure 2.1).

Figure 2.2 shows the varying age groups across the six projects. It can be seen that some projects offered a more homogenous group to be interviewed in terms of age. Differences and similarities between the projects are discussed elsewhere (Chapter 8).

Of the parents and carers, six (7%) were male.

The sample of carers was reasonably diverse in terms of ethnicity (see Figure 2.3). Eighty percent of parents interviewed described themselves as 'UK White' and a further 4% as Irish or 'other' White—Scottish, Welsh and European. Twelve and a half percent described themselves as of dual heritage or Black: African, Caribbean, British or other. There was a small group from the Indian subcontinent.

When we break down the ethnicity of carers by project (Figure 2.4), we see that some service users may be isolated as one of very few from their ethnic group using the project. We can identify projects that appear to have been successful in reaching their local communities. The project set up for Black families in Inner City is also used by White parents and children of mixed heritage, and so it is more ethnically diverse than most of the others. The project at Metropolitan Suburb had made efforts since its inception to research and meet the needs of a variety of groups, and the sample reflected this, with Black and Asian members.

In terms of family size and form (Figure 2.5), the mean (average) family size was 2.4, but there was a significant minority with four or more children.

The 88 parents and carers who were interviewed had a total of 211 children. We asked parents about approximately half (105) of these children, about or for whom they had sought support or advice.

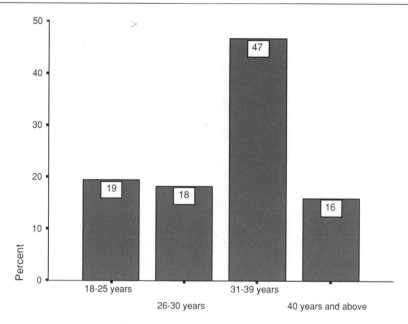

Figure 2.1 Age of primary carer

Children aged under 3 made up 28% of our sample of 105, children between 3 and 10 years old made up nearly half (47%) and the remaining quarter (26%) were young people of secondary school, aged 11–16 years (Figure 2.6).

Just over half (51%) of the parents or carers (women and men) were alone, in the sense of not (in their own view) sharing the main parenting task with a partner. The majority referred to a relationship, but it was not one of consistent joint care of the children. However, some of the partners and their families gave important practical or emotional help to the primary carer. Almost one fifth (18%) were with second or subsequent partners and jointly parented

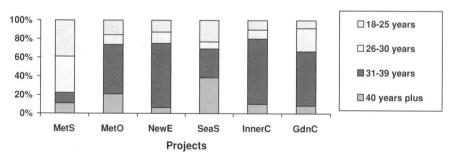

Figure 2.2 Age of carers by project

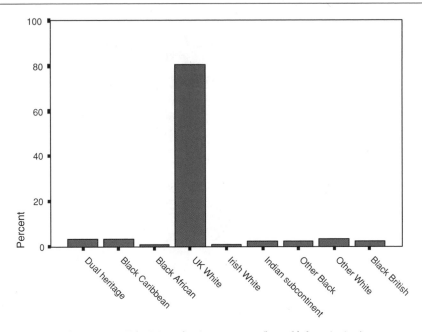

Figure 2.3   Ethnicity of primary carer (by self-description)

children from more than one relationship ('reconstituted families'). A few were in another family form, for example, living with grandparents. Nearly one third (31%) of children were living with both birth parents (Figure 2.7).

There were marked differences between projects with regard to the family form of those parents who were interviewed (though short of statistical significance).

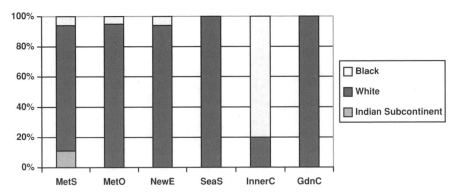

Figure 2.4   Ethnicity of primary carer by project

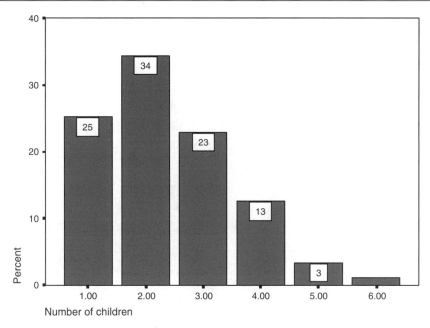

Figure 2.5   Family size (number of children)

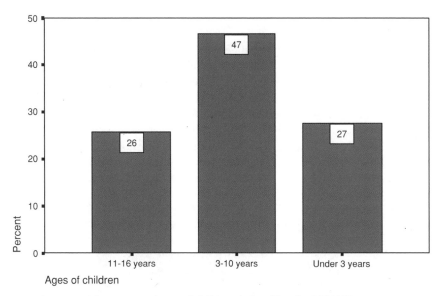

Figure 2.6   Ages of children helped by the NSPCC

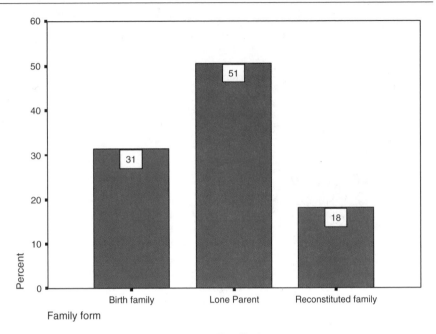

Figure 2.7   Family form

Metropolitan Suburb, Metropolitan Outskirts and New Estate had similar profiles (see Figure 2.8). Garden City had a relatively higher proportion (50%) of reconstituted families, while Sea Side and Inner City had higher proportions—64% and 90% respectively—of lone parents. The projects recognised these profiles, particularly of women parenting alone. In this study, as in other studies (Gibbons and Wilkinson, 1990), family form appears to have a bearing on health and stress and also in relation to children's behavioural difficulties (see p. 35 and p. 51). Projects with a higher proportion of lone parents (Sea Side, Inner City) also had higher levels of family difficulties, but we would need a larger study to test these findings.

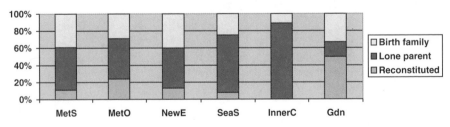

Figure 2.8   Family form by project

Sixteen young people aged seven and over were interviewed in depth and a further 24 were members of group and workshop discussions (40 in all). Of the 16 interviewed, 10 were female, 6 were male and 2 were Black.

SUMMARY

- We interviewed 88 parents or carers, of whom over 90% were female. Most were in their thirties; the age distribution differed in each project sample, but did not appear to be associated with other variables. Just under 20% of parents described themselves as from specific ethnic minority groups; and nearly all of them in just two of the projects.
- Just under half of the 211 children in the sample families were aged between 3 and 10, with the remainder divided about equally between younger infants and adolescents. We interviewed parents concerning half (105) of these children, in relation to whom parents sought support or advice.
- Just over half the parents we interviewed headed one-parent households, although most had a partner who did not share parenting responsibilities. Nearly a third lived with the other parent of their children and the remainder in other family forms, often a second family; occasionally a grandparent was the main carer. Family form also differed across the project samples and there were some patterns here, with the majority of lone parents showing high stress levels. High parental stress was associated with a perception of greater levels of behavioural difficulty in children (see Chapter 3).

3

COMPONENTS OF PARENTAL STRESS

PARENTS' VULNERABILITY IN TERMS OF PAST EXPERIENCE

We asked parents directly about their education, qualifications, age at birth of first child, changes of address, experiences of harm and whether a child had been the subject of child protection enquiries (see Appendix, Measures relevant to the generation and resolution of family problems). A score of 4 out of a possible 12 was our arbitrary cut-off for 'high vulnerability'.

We based the questionnaire on Gibbons' study (Gibbons and Wilkinson, 1990) where vulnerability is rated using six indicators of a possible need for help (which she emphasises could not be seen as predictors of later problems). These were:

- mother under 20 at first birth
- adults not joint parents
- three or more moves in five years
- child protection intervention
- reported violence to parent
- reported criminal record.

In Gibbon's study, scores of more than two suggested 'high vulnerability'. The answers were identified from records and were therefore 'no more than a crude estimate'. The research was influential as a large-scale and carefully designed investigation into aspects of family problems and services to alleviate them. The questions on 'vulnerability' were used because they appeared to identify families under particular stress, although Gibbons advised caution about the findings because the threshold score was arbitrary and the data limited to written records.

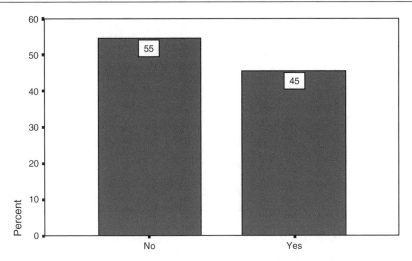

Figure 3.1 Parents ($N = 88$) with high levels of vulnerability at the first interview

Findings on Vulnerability

In this study, high scores on vulnerability at the first interview (see Figure 3.1) were associated with several other issues such as high parental stress ($p = .000$), children's behavioural difficulties ($p = .009$) and perceived low levels of informal support from family and friends ($p = .000$), as well as parents' perceptions of professional support ($p = .038$) *and* their view of the neighbourhood ($p = .008$). Parents who were vulnerable, having combinations of particular adverse past experience and disadvantage, were more likely to have health or stress problems as well as children with perceived behavioural difficulties. They were less likely to feel they had personal or professional support, or to be satisfied with their immediate neighbourhood. These parents were also more likely to assess their child as continuing to have, or to have developed, serious behavioural problems after six months ($p = .035$). Because of the lack of a control group and scientific sampling methods, these findings are not conclusive, but they are consistent with our other findings and merit further work. They are of interest because they indicate associations between a group of background factors and other, current, difficulties and because some of these factors relate to issues of particular concern to the NSPCC, such as family violence.

When vulnerability scores are compared project by project, there is a trend for the highest scores to occur where projects have specific therapy and counselling services dealing with past or present abuse. This reinforces the assertion made by some parents that they had sought out family support services offering relatively easy access to specialist support. Some parents talked about their past experience more readily on the follow-up interview, suggesting that our scores may well be an underestimate.

SOCIAL DISADVANTAGE

We adapted the Index of Social Disadvantage used in Gibbons' study, which showed consistency when tested over the period of that research. The questionnaire asks about such matters as housing tenure, amenities, family size and employment. In Gibbons' study 'the extent of disadvantage among referred couples was significantly greater than among community (non-referred) couples'. There was also a difference between referred and non-referred lone parents, but it was less marked.

Findings on Social Disadvantage

In our study, the majority of householders were not home owners, while in half of the projects the majority had no wage-earner. However, very few of the carers appeared to have severe levels of social disadvantage, although vulnerability was associated with disadvantage at first interview ($p = .001$). This measure needs updating to take account of current credit and hire arrangements since many amenities such as phones and cars had disappeared (or arrived) over the six-month research period (see Figure 3.2).

It was also the case that homes that had similar amenities on paper could be very different to visit. Most had a phone and television, some a car and a few had a personal computer. But some homes also had smashed furniture and fittings, and were chaotic in a far from homely way. These were homes where parental stress and children's behaviour problems were in crisis, and family members referred to the physical deterioration of the home as an added burden.

FINDINGS ON PARENTAL STRESS AND ILL-HEALTH IN THIS STUDY

We used a validated research tool to measure parental stress. This is a list of 24 questions about emotional and physical health, called the Malaise Inventory. It has been used in a number of family support studies (Gibbons et al., 1990; Thoburn et al., 2000). The questionnaire is reproduced in the Appendix. In this study we have called it the Health and Stress Questionnaire.

Well over a third of families (41%) had a critical score of over 7 in terms of parental stress at first interview (see Figure 3.3), suggesting the need for

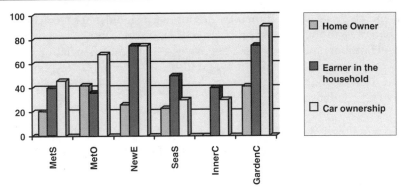

Figure 3.2 Material Assets across the six projects (wage-earner, home ownership, car)

a health assessment and/or treatment. Compared to samples in the other studies using the same measure, this is over twice the rate in non-referred families, but lower than the rate in families referred to social services.

A substantial minority (15% or a sixth) of parents and other carers had scores of 10 or over. Less than 5% had twice the critical score (compared to 15% of parents referred to social services in Thoburn's research). We think this score denotes a major crisis—for instance, one parent in our study was clearly suicidal, one had attempted suicide and suffered permanent internal damage, and another had been hospitalised following serious postnatal depression.

Critical scores did not seem to be associated with the source of referral to the project, for example, a professional or a friend. The association between family

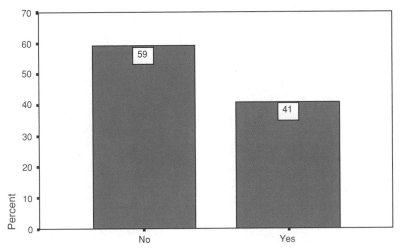

Figure 3.3 Carers ($N = 88$) with severe stress/health problems at the first interview

form and stress or health difficulty did not reach significance ($p = .461$), but lone parents had the greatest proportion of high scores, while second or subsequent families had the smallest. There was a significant association between projects and critical levels of stress and ill-health ($p = .037$). Respondents in Inner City were four times as likely to have severe stress and/or health problems as respondents in New Estate.

Follow-Up after Six Months

The overall direction of change in scores within the follow-up group of 55 parents after six months indicated that parents' scores on stress and health difficulties had shifted. Scores of over half (53%) of the sample had either remained the same (20%), or improved (33%). Nearly half had deteriorated, and almost a quarter (22%) had reached a 'critical' level, that is, a severe level of stress. Taking account of the tendency for higher-scoring individuals to remain in the follow-up, this was still a deterioration overall. There was no significant association between overall changes in stress levels and type of service provision. However, if we look at outcome in relation to the critical score or threshold for concern, we find that a higher proportion of those receiving a structured service (for e.g. regular counselling or a course) attained or maintained lower stress and ill health levels by the end of the six-month period (see Figure 3.4).

In addition to re-administering the Health and Stress Questionnaire after six months, we asked respondents about how they saw changes over this

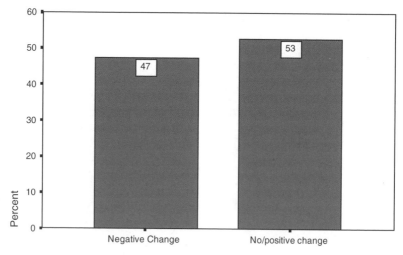

Figure 3.4   Change in stress/health scores over six months

period in a number of areas including health. Their estim
more static than changes as measured by the test scores,
for no change or changes balancing out (48%) and fewer s
(28%) than the test indicated (see table below).

Table 3.1 Changes in health over six months:
comparison of test scores and perceptions

	Changes by test responses (%)	Perceived changes (%)
Worse	48	28
None (or balance out)	19	48
Better	33	24

It appears that specific health questions elicit a sharper picture of carers'
health than do general questions about progress.

Practice Issues: Recognising Spiralling Health and Stress Problems

When problems accumulate, particularly where they include material disadvantage and family conflict without personal or practical support, physical or
mental stresses predictably increase. However, at least in the short to medium
term, receiving outside help does not appear to arrest this negative process for
some of the most stressed parents. In fact, it may well be the case that the effort
of recognising need serious enough to require outside help, and then seeking
help, initially adds to their burden (as suggested by Thoburn's research). The
possibility that structured services, offering parents the opportunity to tackle
specific issues over a period of time, help contain stress should be further
examined. Many of the parents with high stress levels continued to receive
services for over six months.

Parental stress and ill-health deserve more explicit attention in the delivery
of family support. Otherwise parents with severe health and stress problems
may face further costly and traumatic health crises down the road. This un-
dermines their own efforts and those of social work agencies on behalf of
their children, and may lead to unnecessary family breakdown. Although the
Children Act 1989 includes the power to provide services to family members
where this will assist children in need, this has not been used to address parents' health needs systematically. The situation has not improved since we
interviewed parents receiving family support from local authorities a decade
ago (Gardner, 1991). Much more proactive primary health care is needed for
many of these parents and children, who seem to have resigned themselves
to poor health.

Parent's Views about Their Health

A minority of the parents we interviewed were men who were primary carers. Their health scores and profiles were similar to those of women. Men mentioned problems such as serious back pain, agoraphobia and use of anti-depressants.

> *I have pain from a slipped disc and I'm on tablets for anxiety, in the past I was treated for agoraphobia. I would not say I had health problems.*
>
> Father aged 45, four children

Parents with well above the critical scores described chronic and/or disabling conditions, often aggravated by life events. Several described insensitive or neglectful health care as if it were a fact of life and could not be improved.

Both the women quoted below had suffered serious domestic violence and had been accommodated with their children in a women's refuge.

> *I have had very little support from my GP, social services or the hospital's Audiology Department. The hospital told me this is 'progressive' but I need to know more, in case I need other aids in future. My hearing aid does not work, it crackles all the time but they will not change it. And my neighbours complain about the phone being turned up so loud—but I can't get help with that either. I am told the kind of aid I need is too costly.*
>
> Mother aged 30, one child

> *I was diagnosed with multiple sclerosis a few years ago. So far the only symptom I get is my sight goes temporarily in one eye from time to time—it's like a shutter coming down. I found my GP pretty insensitive, although he means well. I overdosed seriously last year and ended up in hospital.*
>
> Mother aged 35, five children

Another mother described her health visitor having to fight for preventive resources:

> *I had serious postnatal depression with my first child and was a psychiatric in-patient. I have had bulimia and borderline agoraphobia but I have got better and more confident and I have weaned myself off the tablets. My GP and health visitor have been very supportive and so has the community psychiatric nurse. The health visitor had to fight for me to get hormone injections after the second child—they cost £26.00 a day for seven days. The hospital would not fund them. Without them I am sure I'd have had another breakdown.*
>
> Mother aged 24, two children

In some areas, a certain fatalism is apparent from both service users and helping agencies—to achieve good health care requires sustained pressure from the patient *and* consistent advocacy. Without it, service users suffer endless delays, inadequate information, poor technical support and were sometimes dismissed as inappropriately demanding—all likely to add to stress on them and their families.

FINDINGS OF OTHER STUDIES ON PARENTAL STRESS AND FAMILY SUPPORT

Figure 3.5 shows recent findings across several studies, showing critical levels of stress and ill-health in parents *not* referred for assistance and in those using various forms of family support. While these populations are not strictly comparable, the findings, as one might expect, show non-referred families as having the least critical stress, those using community-based support intermediate levels of stress, and a high proportion of those referred to social services as having critical stress levels, across four different studies of family support.

Gibbons and her colleagues compared scores at the time of referral and after four months for two groups of carers, a group referred to social services and a comparison group of parents living locally and not referred. The referred group was made up of a sample of parents receiving support from a range of voluntary organisations, and a sample receiving a more 'traditional'

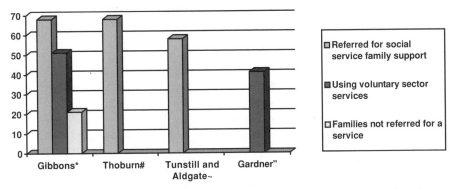

Figure 3.5 Percentage of parents with severe stress/health problems at first interview in four studies of family support services.
Notes:
* Gibbons and Wilkinson's (1990) sample included 72 families referred to and receiving a service from social service (all referrals), 72 referred voluntary sector services, 359 families not referred for a service.
# Thoburn *et al.*'s (2000) sample was 122 families receiving service from social services (including those referred for neglect and emotional harm).
~ Tunstill and Aldgate (2000) included 93 families receiving services from social services (excluding child protection and disabilities).
"Gardner's (this) study is 88 families receiving services from the voluntary sector.
Gibbons, Thoburn and Gardner used the 'malaise inventory' (see Gibbons *et al.*, 1990).
Tunstill and Aldgate interviewed parents about their physical and mental health.

social work service. Parental distress was thought relevant because 'a parent overwhelmed with unpleasant feelings of anxiety and depression is likely to be unable to cope with the ordinary stresses and strains of parenthood, let alone with...serious problems'. The questionnaire also asks about physical symptoms. A score of 7 or more suggests serious difficulties that may need specialist help.

Gibbons and colleagues found that, while the two referred samples showed no significant differences in terms of parental stress at the first interview, there were significant differences between the referred and non-referred 'community' groups. In the two referred groups (in different geographical areas), one subsequently received social work as well as help from local voluntary organisations and one received more traditional social work services, and 51% and 68% of parents respectively had critical scores (seven or more) on the Malaise Inventory. This was true of only 21% of parents in the non-referred group. The authors comment that 'referred parents appeared to be struggling with a much greater burden of anxious and depressed feelings than "ordinary" families with similar aged children'.

Gibbons also asked about family problems that frequently emerged in referral interviews with social workers. Five family problem areas or issues were found in the resulting data: parent–child relationship, social contact, health, finances and relationship with partner. Gibbons found that parental stress was significantly related to each of the five issues. Of the five family problem areas identified, parent–child problems 'made the largest contribution' to stress levels.

Gibbons describes half the sample of families referred to social services as 'lone parents', compared to one in eight of the nonreferred sample, adding that

> the great majority of lone parents were divorced women in their late 20s and early 30s, not single women...reconstituted families—containing children who were not the offspring of both partners jointly—did not appear to be over represented. Social services were attracting the divorced women who had not (or not yet) found another partner.

In this study, by contrast, parents using some of the community-based services included a high proportion of women in new partnerships, including children from previous families ('reconstituted' families).

Parental stress was one of a number of characteristics of the referred sample in Gibbons' research:

> families referred to Social Services in the two areas of the study resembled each other closely in structure and problem levels. However, families who had been randomly selected from similar neighbourhoods were strikingly different. Referred families were more often headed by lone parents. They had more

indicators of social disadvantage and they experienced more financial problems. They appeared less integrated into their neighbourhoods. They had more serious, non-financial, family problems and the main parent was more likely to be emotionally distressed.

Bebbington and Miles (1989) found that a child with a lone parent was eight times more likely to enter local authority accommodation than a child with both parents, and poverty did not account for all of this disparity; but it may be that isolation, ill-health and stress are also influential factors.

Thoburn *et al.* (2000) used the same measure of parental stress with 122 parents who had been referred to social services either because of concerns about possible neglect or emotional harm to their children, or for more general support. They concluded that 'in the weeks after referral... respondents were continuing to experience high levels of stress', approximately two thirds (68%) having levels 'above the conventional cut-off for possible psychiatric disorder' and about one eighth (12%) having levels that were twice the cut-off score, i.e. 'acute distress'. In another recent study of social work with families of children in need (excluding children with a disability and children in need of protection), Tunstill and Aldgate (2000) interviewed parents referred to social services for family support and found that nearly 60% had acute or chronic health problems at first interview.

Other Studies' Follow-Up of Parental Stress Levels

Reinterviewing parents after four months, Gibbons found no association between an improvement in stress levels and social work help in one of the two geographical areas. In the other area, parents who received help from social services were *less* likely to show improvement in stress levels than those who received no service, particularly if they were in a 'high need' group ($p = .009$). This could presumably relate to the type of problem that led to a service being offered, or to the service itself adding to stress levels in the short term.

Certain characteristics of the support system were associated with higher stress at referral—for instance, conflicted relationships and lack of practical support. Having several sources of informal support at the time of referral, particularly practical help, was thought to be the most likely contributory factor to improvement in stress levels. In our study also, informal support appeared to be of primary importance, being associated with improvements in children's behavioural problems after six months, which were in turn associated with parents having good stress and health levels at follow-up (see p. 66 and p. 49).

In the study by Thoburn and colleagues, parents were reinterviewed a year later. Stress levels had become more serious for 10% of the parents re-interviewed, remained the same for 60% and improved for 24%, although a third of those who had improved still had 'marked stress problems'. When all measures of well-being were combined, more families referred for *general* family problems had deteriorated, than had families referred because of specific concerns about neglect or emotional harm, and, perhaps unexpectedly, more of the latter had improved.

Tunstill and Aldgate's study found that over half had a family member with a chronic health problem, and half had regular minor health problems, with depression affecting many. About two thirds of the 93 parents interviewed wanted help with relief of stress. The majority (73%) of these, according to parents' own report, obtained the necessary help from social services, particularly with respect to children's behavioural problems; in cases of parental ill health, more benefits were obtained than had been anticipated.

SUMMARY

- We used a validated health checklist with 88 carers, of whom 55 were followed up after six months. We also asked general questions about health problems and any changes over the six months of the study.
- In this study, well over 40% of carers had a critical stress score (i.e., indicating a level of stress that could warrant a clinical referral) at the first interview. Many carers with critical scores had scored 50% over the critical score. These scores were high, but not as high as in samples referred to social services in other studies. However, there was a significant association between critical scores and project areas, with Inner City's rate over four times that of New Estate. The age of the parents did not appear to account for the differences.
- Parents and carers with critical scores, of both sexes, described a catalogue of chronic physical and psychological problems, punctuated with crises. These included neurological disease, sickle-cell anaemia, cancer, serious back pain, depression, suicide attempts, agoraphobia and eating disorders. In some cases health and stress problems appeared related. A minority of these parents described seriously inadequate or insensitive physical and mental health care, both in hospitals and in the community, and there was thin or non-existent preventive health care in some of the neediest areas.
- Two thirds of those followed up ($N = 55$) had either not improved or had deteriorated on the same health measure. These results have to be treated with caution because the follow-up group was smaller. Proportionally more of those parents who received a structured family support service from NSPCC, maintained or gained a score that was not critical over six months. Overall, respondents' perception of health change was more optimistic than their follow-up test indicated.

PRACTICE POINTS

- Hitherto, few family support providers have *systematically* assessed, or sought to address, the physical and mental health of parents, when they obviously impinge on their parenting capacity—and sometimes not even then.
- We suggest that this may lead to family support efforts being undermined, particularly in the case of 'vulnerable' parents and those with little or no informal support. Some parents who say they are resolving difficulties with children and even 'feel better' overall, actually have *more* symptoms of physical and/or emotional distress after six months. Many are not receiving the health care they need for serious conditions.
- The added stress of acknowledging levels of difficulty that need outside help, then seeking this help and learning new behaviours, needs to be taken into account more fully. Recent findings about the value of informal and practical support such as childcare, financial and domestic help, and the potential of structured, solution-focussed work, are very relevant here.
- A short assessment of *both* parents' health, of the type undertaken for this research, would be a straightforward way of indicating a family's health needs, alongside assessment of the children's health. It is important to remember that 'any service ... may be provided for the family of a particular child in need or *for any member of his family* (our emphasis) if it is provided with a view to safeguarding or promoting the child's welfare' (Children Act 17 (3)). The duty upon health authorities to comply with a reasonable request for help (S27 (3)), and provisions for joint funding under the Health Act 1999, section 31, should be tested further in the joint provision of appropriate preventive health care and family support. The NSPCC has recommended that this element of the Children Act be strengthened (1996).

    These findings are reinforced by other studies and strongly suggest that joint health and social services plans for strategic service development should more actively and consistently address parents' physical and mental health needs. This would buttress family support initiatives.

4

CHILDREN AND FAMILY SUPPORT

This chapter describes difficulties with particular children that often brought their parents to the NSPCC's projects for help, and the changes that had occurred when we re-interviewed parents six months later. Pecora *et al.* (1995) note that while

> improvement of child functioning is an implicit goal of family based programs, ... many (programs) focus evaluation efforts on documenting outcomes for families, collecting relatively little data on outcomes for individual children (other than placement). (Pecora *et al.*, 1995)

Behavioural difficulties are a major source of family strain. Gibbons (1991) found that parent–child problems made the largest contribution to stress levels of all family difficulties. Behavioural problems or risk of offending accounted for some 20% of children who were accommodated in 1999–2000 (Department of Health, 2001).

FAMILY SUPPORT SERVICES FOR CHILDREN

The six NSPCC family support projects all offered support to parents in dealing with children's behaviour that presented difficulties, without using physical or emotional punishment. The aims were to reduce stress on parents by offering alternative responses, and to reduce the risk of significant harm to children from parents who had already used excessive discipline or who feared they might do so. Methods included skills training, group work and counselling or advice sessions, with or without home visits. Many projects worked directly with the child as well, using a similar range of methods. Some projects were experimenting with approaches such as video home guidance, where video 'clips' of parent–child interactions are used to reinforce positive and effective parenting behaviours. Family support activities and the views of family members are detailed in Chapter 5, Typologies of Family Difficulties, and in Chapter 8, Examples of Family Support Practice.

THE CHILDREN IN THE STUDY

We asked parents and carers about 105 children who had either made direct use of NSPCC's family support, or whose parents had received a service in order to assist them with parenting. These 105 made up half of the 211 children in the sample families. Fully tested questionnaires were completed on the 76 children aged three years and over. One of these tools, the Strengths and Difficulties questionnaire, is reproduced in the Appendix (Methodology). In brief, it is a practical assessment tool, 'a brief behavioural screening questionnaire that provides balanced coverage of children and young people's behaviours, emotions and relationships... designed to meet the needs of researchers, clinicians and educationalists' (Goodman, 1997). It has also been incorporated into the Framework for Assessment of Children in Need (Department of Health, 1999) for social workers—this research provided a 'field test' of its use.

We also looked for changes in children's behaviour and in the strengths and difficulties they presented to their parents over the six months of family support intervention.

We could not directly attribute the changes we found to a particular intervention, but were interested in measurable and observed change and in patterns that would merit further attention.

While our main source of information about children's behaviour over the six-month period was the 88 primary carers, we recognised that 'no one type of information typically provides the same data as any other type' (Achenbach et al., 1987). We obtained a useful group of 14 assessments from teachers and 16 from children, using the same questionnaire, which is provided in a number of formats. In a small group of cases, these responses were used to compare different points of view on the same child.

The screening tool asks questions about specific behaviours indicating children's positive social (pro-social) behaviour, peer relations, hyperactivity, conduct and emotional state. Five additional questions about the type, degree and effect(s) of any difficulty on the family provide a summary of the respondent's views.

We asked these summarising questions, which were not scored, of parents and health visitors about children below the age of three. The findings are broadly consistent with those for older children. For children aged three and over, a threshold or critical score identifies children who may be at risk of more severe problems. We used the higher of two possible thresholds, for use

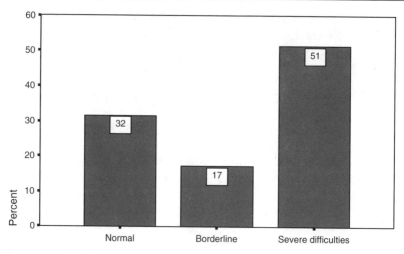

Figure 4.1 Children's behaviour: Strengths and difficulties (Goodman, 1997)

with a relatively 'low risk' sample, in order, as far as possible, to avoid scoring children incorrectly as having difficulties. A 'higher risk' sample would be a group of children using an adolescent mental health service, for instance. Because our sampling methods were not scientific, the findings should be treated with caution.

FINDINGS ON CHILDREN'S BEHAVIOURAL DIFFICULTIES

As assessed by parents and carers at the first interview, over two thirds (68%) of children aged three and over, receiving family support either directly or via their parents, had a borderline (17%) or critical (51%) score, using the higher threshold (see Figure 4.1). There is a significant positive relationship between age of the child and degree of difficulty at first interview. Older children show greater difficulty, having higher scores on the behavioural questionnaire ($p = .014$).

Parents saw the majority of these children (69%) as having normal levels of pro-social behaviours, for example, helpfulness and care of younger children.

A cluster analysis was used to determine combinations of traits. (For a discussion of this method of analysis, see Gibbons, 1991). There were three such groupings: the first (42%) with fewer difficulties on this measure, a second group (the largest, at 45%) with hyperactivity and conduct difficulties and a smaller group (13%) with emotional and peer relationship difficulties,

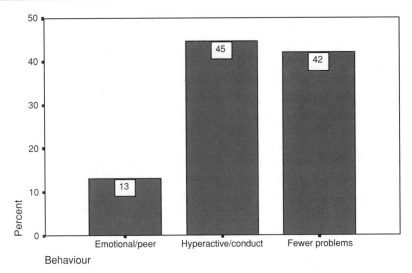

Figure 4.2 Most frequent combinations of children's strengths and difficulties (cluster analysis)

as well as some hyperactivity (see Figure 4.2). These groupings do not vary significantly by age or gender.

We were interested in violence or threats of violence between children, as parents and children expressed much anxiety on this score. Nearly half of the parents thought their children were being bullied and nearly as many thought they were fighting or bullying others. There was an appreciable, though not statistically significant, overlap between the two groups with over half of the children who were possible fighters or bullies also seen by their parents as being bullied. Figure 4.3 shows graphically the overlap between groups of children who often or sometimes fight or bully others, and those who are themselves perceived to be bullied to a greater or lesser degree.

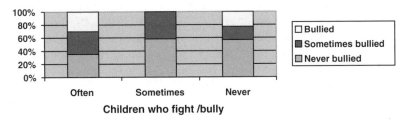

Figure 4.3 The relationship between bullying and being bullied

Difficulties in School

The small group of fourteen teachers from mainstream schools who were interviewed gave a profile of children's behaviour that was similar to that given by their parents. Half the children we asked teachers about were given a critical score and another fifth (21%) a borderline score. Teachers were generally very good respondents with a detailed memory of individual children. Some studies suggest that while both parents and teachers give valid descriptions of children's behaviour, teachers' descriptions are more reliable indicators of outcomes. (Achenbach, 1991; Glisson, 1996). Teachers gave us evidence of severe difficulties in school with the children we were studying; for example, one described a 15-year-old boy hammering nails into his shoes and kicking other children with them, and another described a girl aged 14 who bullied and was enuretic and aggressive.

Most of the 16 young people with whom we used the questionnaire saw themselves as having behavioural or other problems, though not as severe as indicated in their parents' assessments. Despite this they all saw themselves as having normal positive social behaviour as well.

Children's Difficulties at Different Ages

We asked parents of all age groups questions about the degree of any difficulty and the amount and duration of stress it imposed. Of children aged under three, 44% were thought to have difficulties and about a quarter of these (11%) were 'definite'. A substantial minority of parents with concerns about this age group thought that the difficulties distressed the child (41%), as well as caused the parent herself/himself stress (33%), and/or interfered with life at home (18%). There was some overlap between these categories.

Assessed in this way, in terms of its immediate effects of stress on the child and family, difficulty differed significantly with age, with over half of children over three seen as having 'definite difficulties' ($p = .000$). There is a significant positive relationship between the age of the child and perception of stress or 'burden' ($p = .026$). The mean age of children found to be a 'burden' is 9 years, whereas the mean age of children *not* seen in this way is 6.7 years. It seems that a change in many parents' perceptions occurs in the junior school age range, with increasing awareness of the child's distress and effects of her/his behaviour within and outside the family.

There was no statistical difference in the spread of children's strengths and difficulties across the six research projects, but there were clear patterns similar to those for stress and ill health (see Figure 4.4). In Inner City, only about a sixth (15.4%) of the sample was seen by parents as having lower levels of difficulty, whereas over half (61.5%) was seen thus at New Estate.

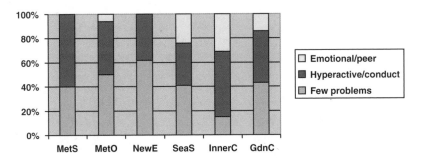

Figure 4.4 Most frequent combinations of children's strengths and difficulties by project

Taken together, these findings suggest that it is possible to map the degree, extent and type of difficulty that children are struggling with, and for which parents seek help and advice. This will clearly improve individual assessments. If aggregated, this type of data can also assist in strategic planning to provide more sensitive services to particular groups as needs change over time and/or in different settings; for example, such data would be extremely useful in the early stages of a Best Value review of services for vulnerable children.

Follow-Up over Six Months

We used several methods of measuring change in behavioural problems. We looked for changes within the entire follow-up group, and also looked at whether children maintained or attained a level of difficulty that was below the critical threshold, that is, not severe, over the six-month period.

We followed up 47 of the original sample of 76 children (61%) after six months, using the same questionnaire. Within the group, there was a change in scores with 58% improving, 7% the same and the remainder (35%) deteriorating, in their parents' assessment (see Figure 4.5). While the data does not allow for a causal explanation of these changes, we found various associated factors—parental stress, vulnerability and levels of informal support—which merit further investigation.

Parents and Children with Difficulties over Six Months

We considered children's behavioural outcomes after six months in terms of the threshold score (see Figure 4.6). We found that if children's behaviour scores had stayed at, or improved to a point below, the critical level, then the carer's stress level is also more likely to be within the normal range after six months ($p = .026$).

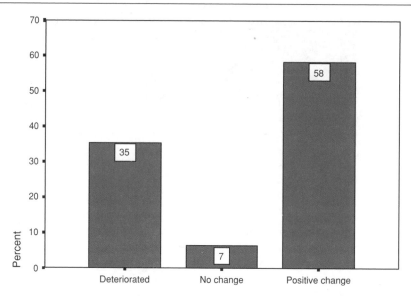

Figure 4.5 Changes in strengths and difficulties scores over six months

Parents with greater vulnerability at the first interview were more likely to assess their child as having behavioural difficulties ($p = .009$), and as continuing to have, or to have developed, serious behavioural problems by the end of the six-month period ($p = .035$). Vulnerability of the parent appeared to be associated with poorer outcomes on children's behaviour in relation to the threshold for concern.

When we profile these two factors (parent's vulnerability and children's behaviour after six months) across the six projects, there is again a recognisable

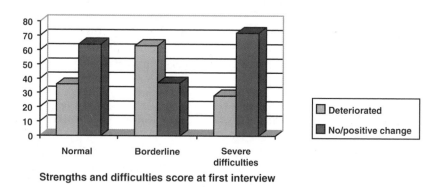

Figure 4.6 Positive/negative outcomes on strengths and difficulties scores over six months

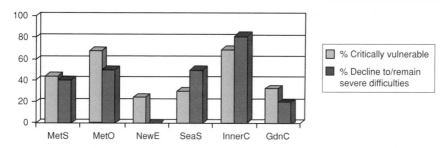

Figure 4.7 Percentage of vulnerability in project compared with changes in strengths and difficulties scores

pattern that appears to reinforce these findings (Figure 4.7). Vulnerability has been discussed in Chapter 3 (p. 32) and includes experience of harm or violence, multiple changes of address and parenthood at a young age. We found it to be associated with perceived levels of informal support at the first interview ($p = .000$); those who presented themselves as less vulnerable had higher levels of informal support.

Supportive Networks and Children's Behaviour

Networks of support are discussed more fully in Chapter 6. Informal support and neighbourhood rating are separately associated with children's behavioural outcomes. Parents with more informal supports from friends and relatives were more likely to see children maintain or improve to a non-critical score ($p = .000$), and this was more so if they had a positive view of the immediate neighbourhood ($p = .005$). The reverse was also the case; the fewer their informal supports and the more negative parents' rating of their neighbourhood, the more likely they were to assess their child as maintaining, or deteriorating to, a score suggesting more serious behavioural problems. In these findings, the most influential factor on children's behaviour appears to be informal support.

OTHER FINDINGS

Additionally, there were some patterns, short of significance, that are consistent with our other findings. For instance, there was a pattern of younger children showing more improvement ($p = .234$). There was also a pattern of children in 'second' or reconstituted families showing more improvement in behaviour than did children in either birth families or living with lone parents. ($p = .24$). This did not appear to relate to the age of the parent. Carers in these second families also had relatively low levels of critical stress. The reasons for this are not clear, but it is possiblè that parents in second families who attend the projects are highly motivated with regard to prevention of further family breakdown.

Children's Behaviour across the Projects

There are strong variations, again short of statistical significance, in the degree of children's behavioural improvement across projects, but no clear association between improvements and type of service. The highest levels of improvement took place at New Estate and Metropolitan Suburb. Both these projects focussed on parents with younger children and both had some of the most structured and theoretically based services for these groups. It may be that our measures picked up the behavioural improvements they sought to achieve. Metropolitan Outskirts and Garden City were in the middle ground, with more children improving than otherwise. Both work with under fives *and* older age groups. Sea Side and Inner City projects had the highest proportion of children either not improving or deteriorating. One possible reason is that these projects do more direct work with older children referred by Social Services, whose problems are unlikely to alleviate over six months. Even so, in the view of the parents we reinterviewed, the behaviour of between 28% of the children (in Inner City) and 50% (in Sea Side) *had* improved. Children we reinterviewed thought that the projects had helped them to maintain or form relationships, particularly with friends with fewer problems.

SUMMARY

- Because our sampling method was not scientific, these findings are tentative.
- We used a tested questionnaire to ask parents and carers about 76 children aged over three; their social behaviour, peer relationships, conduct and emotional state. Straightforward questions about degree, duration and effects of any difficulties were also asked about these children, and additionally, about 29 children under three. All these 105 children received family support, either directly by attending projects and/or indirectly because the parent or carer sought specific help and advice concerning them. They made up approximately half of the 211 children in the households.
- Over two thirds of the children over three had severe or borderline problems and older children had more difficulties ($p = .014$). The most frequent cluster of difficulties was hyperactivity and conduct problems (45%), and

in this group the types of difficulty did not vary significantly by age or gender.

- Bullying was a major problem, with nearly half of the parents thinking their child was bullied or else fighting and bullying others—and half of these thought the child had both experiences. The picture obtained from small groups of teachers and young people was not markedly different from that obtained from parents.

- Nearly five times as many parents of children over three saw the child as having 'definite' difficulties as did parents of younger children. Age relates significantly to how much stress (or 'burden') older children are seen to impose. There appears to be a cut-off point around age nine when children's difficulties become more likely to be seen as distressing to the child and problematic for others.

- There were differences between projects in both degree and pattern of children's behavioural difficulties.

- We followed up 47 of the older children and 15 of the children under three after six months. For children over three there was significant improvement in behavioural difficulties over six months, as assessed by the parents. As expected, degree of improvement in children's behaviour was negatively associated with the earlier degree of difficulty, i.e. children who had the most difficulties at the first interview improved the least.

- Where children's behaviour had been maintained at or improved to a point below the critical score, i.e. did not give serious concern, this was significantly associated with good parental health and well being at the second interview, but we cannot identify the cause and effect here. Children's behaviour at the second interview was also associated with the parents' vulnerability in terms of past experiences, the most vulnerable parents seeing least improvement, and with levels of informal support parents received from family and friends.

- Generally speaking, and again short of statistical significance, the fewer the children who had severe difficulties in a project, the greater the improvement for them *and* for other children who had fewer difficulties.

- The research did not allow us to associate specific circumstances or interventions with improvements in behaviour, but there were some interesting patterns that merit further examination. The most successful projects appeared to be those using theoretically based, structured approaches with children and their parents, but these approaches may simply be more amenable to evaluation.

- Overall, the findings merit further investigation with a larger, more rigorously selected sample.

PRACTICE POINTS

- It seems to be both practicable and necessary to assess the profile of children's behaviour regularly, both for individuals and for groups of children to whom family support is or may be offered. This will allow for better-targeted and more efficient use of skills and resources, particularly across health, education and social services.
- Adults who experience children's behaviour as a burden said that help in dealing with their own symptoms of stress assisted them in dealing more sensitively with this behaviour.
- Parents are transferring learning about how to manage younger children to apply it to their older children with difficulties. Projects that provided structured services for this age group as well as for their parents and younger children in the family appeared to be effective in preventing deterioration. This work has cost implications, in terms of training staff and buying in specialist advice, but the flexibility it offered was in stark contrast to rigid age and eligibility criteria applied by most services; these criteria selected out some children as 'less needy' without effective follow-up.
- The need for improved access to preventive mental health services for older children is an issue of major concern to parents and professionals in all the research locations. The uneven spread of these services, and their inadequacy in areas of greatest need, is discussed in the final chapter.
- In the next chapter (Typologies of family difficulties), we give accounts of children's depression and/or violence, which were corroborated by parents and staff. Many of them were not receiving the specialist help that they urgently needed, despite the government's investment in these services.

5

TYPOLOGIES OF FAMILY DIFFICULTIES

Looking for patterns in the data we found it possible to group children according to a preliminary typology. This chapter introduces and illustrates the typology. It is firstly, *children with fewer difficulties*; secondly, *children who are isolated or anxious*; thirdly, *overburdened children*; and lastly, *children who are at risk of social exclusion through challenging behaviour*. This is intended to clarify the data; it is not exclusive and we have included examples that do not obviously fit the groups. Children often fell into more than one group, but one aspect of their difficulties was predominant.

We also give examples of what service users had to say about children for whom they requested family support, who made up approximately half of the 211 children in the families we studied. The quotations from parents and children illustrate issues raised in other chapters, for example children's behaviour and parents' stress.

Most parents linked their child's problems to their own, and talked about both. The great majority did not see the child as the primary or only cause of their stress. Whether or not they saw the child as having a difficulty, they still had aspirations for him or her. Both the mothers and fathers we spoke to wanted their children to make friends and be able to socialise, as well as to make progress at school.

While school achievement to the best of the child's ability was very important to the majority of parents, equally important was the child's self-esteem, whether or not he or she achieved. One parent said 'whatever happens to them now, they will have with them for the rest of their lives, so I want her to get rid of the bad things that have happened and enjoy the rest of her childhood'.

- *Children with fewer difficulties.* These were mostly, but not all, pre-school children. Parents wanted them to be able to play and later to socialise on equal terms, in other words, to gain a positive social identity and the ability to assert this without victimising or becoming a victim. They saw this as a prerequisite to good learning at school *and* as important in itself.

- *Isolated children.* These were children who were anxious, insecure, sometimes bullied, and in some cases had been abused. Their self-esteem was low and they found it difficult to make and/or keep friends. They included children who refused school, were depressed and had eating or sleeping problems. In some cases they also had conduct difficulties.
- *Overburdened children.* Some children had become isolated because they were coping for other family members, and were carrying adult responsibilities. Externally, these children sometimes covered up their problems and often appeared to function well socially. Emerging difficulties, such as school non-attendance, might go unnoticed. At another level, they were also often isolated, already suffering severe stress, and unhappy.
- *Children at risk of social exclusion.* These children's behaviour had set them apart but had at least gained some notice for their difficulties and often spurred a parent to get preventive help, both for the child in question, for a younger child and/or for the parent herself/himself. They were often victims of emotional harm by witnessing extreme violence and/or, in some cases, being physically or verbally abused by a parent or sibling or by peers. The child hid her or his isolation and lack of self-worth in defiant, angry behaviour and/or running away. Occasionally, they were part of a group of friends perceived as anti-social. They were often on waiting lists or being assessed for professional assistance. Because of their difficulties in attending and using the sessions, they often 'dropped out' of therapy.

These theoretical groups of isolated, overburdened and potentially excluded children can overlap. A child might be described as quiet, isolated and overburdened at home but aggressive at school.

PARENTS' NETWORKS

Parents and carers described themselves as having a range of adult relationships and networks similar to that described above. These ranged from secure and/or extensive networks, through less secure relationships, to isolation, or to relationships characterised by hostility. The role that parents ascribed to the family support project appeared to relate to how confident they were in their other relationships and networks.

We therefore suggest another typology; firstly, parents who see family support as an *extension* of a pre-existing network; secondly, parents for whom it supplies a *bridge* to form a social network, for instance, for newcomers to an area; and thirdly, parents for whom it is a *substitute* network during a period of transition or crisis. Again, these three groupings are not static.

- *Parents with an extended network.* These parents had lived in the area for some time, were reasonably happy there, and/or had maintained a full social network of friends and relatives. They had little difficulty in approaching professionals or in getting help to do so if necessary. For them, the NSPCC project was one element in, and an extension of, their wider social network. At a first glance, it could appear that some of this group were "passengers" who were using the project without really needing it. In many cases they were survivors—parents who had earlier come through extreme isolation following abuse or a similar trauma. For other parents they provided a model that no professional without similar experiences could achieve—'I have been there and you can get through this'. They often gave their time free to the project and/or went on to gain qualifications and paid work in a related field. Some parents thought that they were still vulnerable. One such parent said, 'I keep in touch both for my grandchild and myself—I know I can have a chat if I get low'.
- *Parents whose networks were patchy or insecure.* These might have a strong partner or friendship at the personal level, but be new to the community or isolated in it; or the reverse, have work and community contacts but might have recently separated and/or might be at war with the family. For these partly or recently isolated parents, the project was a bridge or springboard from which they repaired or reconstructed the missing part of the network: made friends, gained confidence to socialise, sought educational or leisure experience, attained qualifications or work, and/or obtained the professional help they needed.
- *Parents whose networks were thin or poor.* These could be described as socially excluded in that they had no or very few positive and consistent relationships. There might be volatile partnerships that ended in rejection with or without violence, friendships followed by enmity with neighbours, help followed by perceived intrusion from professionals and conflict with other agencies. For these families, who were often in great distress, the project provided a temporary *substitute network* and a *safe haven*. They needed a respite in order to address a life crisis or the more chronic issues it represented. These were often compounded by long standing self-neglect, inability to obtain entitlements or positive assistance (as opposed to problem-specific interventions), apprehension at their children's increasingly desperate behaviour, and sheer exhaustion. Sometimes they had to learn or to re-learn (alongside their children) basic relationships of trust, how to play and how to set boundaries.

Children's and parents' positions in these typologies were not obviously related, although as we have seen in previous chapters, high levels of vulnerability and lack of personal support did relate to several other areas of difficulty. The rest of this chapter illustrates (using quotations that have been made anonymous by changing any identifying details) situations frequently dealt with by the family support projects.

ISOLATED CHILDREN

Andrea, aged 13, had been abused by a male relative. She said:

> my mum got in touch with NSPCC and Social Services and NSPCC are taking him to court. I don't feel secure to go into a group and that includes school so they got me a home tutor. I talk to (staff member NSPCC) and it helps me sort out my feelings. I am up and down a bit. I'd like to come for as long as it takes. I'd like to not get as angry and to understand my emotions within myself so I don't take it out on my mum.

Her mother commented:

> Social Services referred us here and at first I was worried but now I think it is very good. The investigation was quite frightening and so the practical support here has helped us through. For instance, they got her back into education. She used to be confident, and then suddenly became very introverted and frightened. She was often sick—could not keep even water down—then frightened to go to school. So they organised a home tutor on the basis of what NSPCC told them, using their assessment. I know she can phone here if she needs to talk things through, and they have given me advice how to handle her if she has a strop on—not to get into a shouting match but give her time out, some space—it has worked. I dread to think where we'd be without this help.

OVERBURDENED CHILDREN

Joanna, aged twelve, said she felt more relaxed at the project than at school because she was busy but not pressurised:

> I have lived here all my life and come to the NSPCC young people's group for two years. I help taking the children (siblings six, four and two years old) to school and making sure they are safe. My mum comes here with them and they have activities so I can have my group too. I wanted to make friends and be included in the conversation. That has happened. You learn things but you don't have to be quiet all the time. My lisp was my big problem and they ragged me so I started to skip school. Mum took me down the police station and NSPCC came and phoned the school. It has stopped now. What we do here helps with school because you have to work as a team.

Her mother spoke of similar extended support but with an element of challenge, which she thought had made her negotiate and listen more:

> NSPCC have reassured me, like having a big mum. But they give you a different point of view—it's critical support. If I argue with my husband, they'll stand in the middle.

I've noticed Joanna more. I think she's very bright and I want her to do better than I have, so I'm going to get her into the best school around here.

Six months later Joanna's mother reported that she had changed school and was making good progress.

CHILDREN AT RISK OF SOCIAL EXCLUSION AND EMOTIONAL HARM

A teacher described this 11-year-old as a child who had caused her great concern:

Laura gets into a state when the other children are cruel and she does the same to them. She can go through the entire school system on a bad day. She's a bit of a mess—not really with it sometimes. Her mother was very keen for her to do all the after school activities because her partner works nights and she said she wanted to be alone with him. We get very little outside help for children like Laura and when (NSPCC worker) visited her once a week it did wonders for her.

Laura's mother felt trapped by the family's needs, and tried to understand her daughter's problems:

NSPCC are there for you and come around if you phone. Laura's attitude hasn't really improved. She's bullied and called 'smelly'. She still wets her pants a bit and hides them from me. The GP says there's nothing physically wrong and she will grow out of it. I guess she may have been anxious when she was small. Her brother's father used to head butt me and smash my head on the wall. They both saw it. The screaming, all that. She thought (he) was her father but she knows now—I never really knew her dad. My partner tries his best but they argue with him so much he's losing patience and I'm afraid he'll leave.

This example of a family crisis involving Jake, aged 11, and described by his mother, indicates the fine line for some children between success and disaster.

Jake goes to his dad for the weekend and comes back wound up—his dad is very angry because I left and am with another man. Jake gets into violent tempers and has broken all the stair rods, the door panels and most of the chairs. Social Services said there was nothing they could do. The GP got me to Child Psychology and they treated me like I was totally in the wrong—'do you think you are to blame for the way he is? Do you think if you stopped fighting your husband, that Jake would be ok'? I think Jake got hold of some speed because he was behaving oddly and in the middle of the night I woke up and he had a kitchen knife to my throat. I managed to talk to him and I called the police, then Social Services got the NSPCC around.
Jake sees (NSPCC worker) regularly and they do activities—Jake thinks the world of him. He holds his temper better—goes for a bike ride. I can talk to him now. Jake told

me that he would have killed me, because he wanted someone to blame and that his dad said he should have done it.

Jake's teacher saw a different side of him, with the potential to succeed;

Jake has a few absences, but far less than in the past. He has worked very hard and his maths is improving. I don't see him as having any difficulties in school.

PARENTS WITH AN EXTENDED NETWORK

Margaret abused alcohol and at times behaved erratically, abandoning her two children under five years old, but friends and family had rallied to help:

My partner and my parents have helped, so has the doctor and health visitor and my college tutor. Everyone has tried. I've got an alcohol problem and I walked out on the children—they were taken away overnight. NSPCC showed they genuinely care, they did not judge me but they helped me negotiate with my mum and dad who have a Residence Order. Peter's behaviour is very difficult. They've helped to get him diagnosed as having attention deficit disorder; hopefully he will get some help.
Margaret aged 25, mother of two including Peter aged 5

After six months, her partner had left her. She had temporarily left the area and taken a major overdose. At the follow-up interview she said:

I wanted to leave everything—I still don't really want the responsibility of the children, but I see them every week. The NSPCC people here kept in touch all through—sent me cards while I was in hospital, and I phoned them. They have had to get the police to escort me off the premises here but they have not given up on me. I have been given a second chance and I can see a future. I've not had a drink for twelve weeks. NSPCC are one of the very few places that have put up with me through thick and thin.

Anita was a grandmother with three adult children and six grandchildren. The project had helped her, she said, to extend her network and to apply her skills:

I work part time as a school meals assistant and I have strong links with the church, so I think there is a lot of support for me. But I come to NSPCC as well, because my granddaughter needs help—she has been very difficult since my daughter's marriage split up. And I still need help—I first came to NSPCC when I was in my daughter's position. My other children are doing fine, and I think my grandchildren will be ok if they can get help now. I help as a volunteer, with fund raising and I help with Social Services' training as well. Sometimes I get low and I know I can talk to someone here. I call it keeping me on an even keel.

PARENTS WITH A PATCHY NETWORK

David was a father of three who was bringing up the children alone and felt very isolated:

My children were returned to me by the courts when my ex-wife's partner abused them. He locked my son in the loft and peed on his food. Fortunately, Social Services found out. Then I remarried and my wife didn't get on with my eldest, I had no idea. I came home one day and he was hiding in the toilet, she had attacked him with a kitchen knife. He covered up but I got it out of her and that was the end of that—we divorced and I'm alone. I'm in touch with my ex-wife's mother and Social Services, but otherwise hardly anyone around here. NSPCC got involved when Social Services asked me to supervise contact with their mother and I said no. They have done some wonderful work to help the children understand what happened. I can't wait for Thursdays when the drop-in happens because it is so enjoyable to get out.
David, father with children aged 15, 8 and 6 years

After six months this father had started to make friends locally.

PARENTS WITH NO, OR A CONFLICTED, NETWORK

Mary was desperate because she was at odds with both relatives and neighbours and friends:

because we are poor we don't look smart and we are not accepted. Only parents who are working can afford new clothes. David has taken the house apart, he breaks windows. The neighbour climbed over the fence, and gave him a hiding because he killed his pet rabbit. David has just told me he's been abused by my best friend's partner—I can't believe it. It means we can't go there—she won't speak to me. And my sister has stopped visiting. Apart from NSPCC there is no one. (NSPCC worker) got me to the community psychiatric nurse, who is very supportive. And they have interviewed David, he will get a social worker. At the moment I feel like when it is night, dark—nothing out there. I feel like I have lost my enjoyment in life and want it always to be like that, darkness—nothing.

After six months, Mary was overcoming her agoraphobia. David (age 10) had shown some benefit from medication, but this was now 'wearing off' after 3 to 4 hours. At school he was seen to have major problems of hyperactivity, aggression and stealing, and exclusion was being considered. Over the six months, the NSPCC had helped Mary to keep in touch with the project by taking her there. NSPCC's family support workers had visited David regularly. However, this NSPCC family support project was due to have its funding withdrawn by the local authority; this led to its subsequent closure.

SUMMARY

- Looking for patterns in the data, we have grouped children and young people as follows; those with fewer problems (generally younger children); children who are isolated or anxious; children at risk of social exclusion and isolation because of their own behaviour and children who are overburdened with responsibilities. These categories are not mutually exclusive.
- Parents and carers fall into a further set of groups: those with a secure and/or extended network; those with an insecure or incomplete network and those with very few and/or very poor relationships.
- The two typologies are not obviously related, although lack of a good informal support network appears to relate to other areas of difficulty including children's behaviour (see the next chapter).

PRACTICE POINTS

- The NSPCC offers preventive family support to children and parents in crisis. For instance, counselling of the child and the non-abusive parent, following child abuse; for children being bullied; for children who have witnessed violence in the home; for children who present a risk to others; for children whose parent is at risk for psychiatric or emotional reasons.
- Family support services that are sufficiently flexible can adapt to specific family needs by offering an extension to an existing network, *or* a bridge to other types of support, *or* a temporary substitute network while family members dealt with serious problems. Children report using a similar range of support, depending on the extent of their needs.
- Family support services that include staff with specialist training (for instance, in child protection, in dealing with children's behavioural difficulties) can offer an initial assessment of need. Where good professional networks exist, they can also speed up access to other support services. These include education (home tuition, staff dealing with bullying, home–school liaison, educational psychology); social services (child protection case conferences, contact arrangements, court proceedings) and health (community psychiatric services, child mental health services).
- They can help parents maintain or re-negotiate crucial links not only with services but with the extended family after a disruption, or with partners where stable contact arrangements would benefit a child.
- Parents and referring agencies were very clear that without access to the projects, children in families who were in crisis, with few other supports, were at risk of significant emotional harm, mental ill-health or family breakdown.

6

SUPPORT NETWORKS IN THE COMMUNITY

This chapter investigates sources of support available to the parents and carers whom we have described in earlier chapters. Layers of support closest to parents included partners, children, the extended family and friends. Beyond them lay various community resources, including the NSPCC. We have described how the research related the NSPCC family support work to other strands of support in the community in order to profile different communities' needs and support networks. Research methods included:

- a quantitative profile of the community using census and local authority data
- in-depth interviews with selected families to look in detail at their formal and informal support networks
- interviews with key informants from various agencies about their perception of the community's needs in relation to preventive services.

In subsequent chapters, we use data collected for local and central government to describe communities from a 'top down' perspective. This chapter takes a more personal approach and brings together the views of parents, carers and local professionals who have used the NSPCC's family support projects, as well as those of NSPCC staff. They identified types and levels of support available in the community. The results support the view that positive networks of friends and family are of paramount importance in creating neighbourhoods perceived as safer, more resilient and more rewarding to live in with regard to child-rearing. Resources alone cannot substitute for these networks but a crucial role of family support is to both make use of and promote them.

We devised 'Networks' and 'Community Leader' questionnaires. The first was for service users and the second for staff and volunteers working in local agencies. Both questionnaires were administered by the researcher, with notes taken during the interview. The first part of both the questionnaires asks the interviewee to define the area local to the project by name and to rate aspects such as appearance, safety and friendliness. Interviewees could compare it to the area they lived in, if different. These questions were adapted from a survey conducted as part of an American study (Garbarino and Kostelny, 1992). That study questioned why two 'areas with similar socioeconomic profiles may have very different rates of child maltreatment' and 'undertook a small set of interviews to illuminate the important but elusive variable of community climate'.

Garbarino and colleagues studied the meaning of 'risk' in relation to areas where there are high, or higher than expected, rates of child abuse. They conclude that a high-risk area for children was found to be 'socially impoverished' in broader terms (Garbarino and Sherman, 1980). For instance, it offered more stressful day-to-day social interaction for families, including that with neighbours. Conclusions from this survey were that in one area there were strong informal community networks and in the other, though similar socioeconomically, there was much more dissociation from such networks on the part of both staff and service users. This area also suffered much higher abuse rates and double the child death rate of the other. Taken together, these findings

> suggest an important reality about neighbourhood life: social momentum is a powerful force. When things are going badly, the tendency is for all the social systems to be pulled down together. It takes extraordinary energy and effort to resist such negative social momentum. (Garbarino and Kostelny, 1992)

Our findings on services for children in need in authorities with a reactive rather than a strategic response to human crises, tend to reinforce this view (see Chapter 9).

We asked 88 parents and carers using NSPCC services, similar questions about their neighbourhoods across the six projects that we studied indepth. Thirty-seven staff members from various local agencies, including the NSPCC (Figure 6.1), were also questioned about the degree and type of child

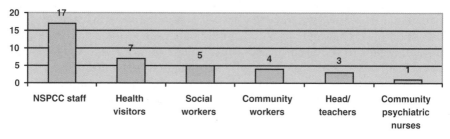

Figure 6.1 Professionals interviewed about support networks ($N = 37$)

protection concerns, advantages and disadvantages for families living in the neighbourhood and which local agencies or individuals offered support.

For service users, there was also a section asking about the support that the carer obtained. Support was divided into three levels: *informal* (family and friends); *semi-formal* (groups, clubs or activities including NSPCC, and voluntary or paid work); and *formal* (agencies such as health and social services). Carers had no problems with these 'levels' or with identifying the amount of support received (none, a little, or a lot). We also obtained examples of various types of support. The first two sections of the questionnaire were scored.

The final section asked service users and agency staff about the NSPCC project. This included their views about NSPCC as an agency, their access route to the service, type of service and length of use, and its perceived effectiveness to date in relation to their expectations. Parents were asked about the most important functions of the project, and its meaning for them, in their own words. This questionnaire was used with 88 service users in the first round and 55 in the six-month follow-up.

We used the term 'community climate' for the sum of a respondent's views about the area in which she or he lived and the support they could rely on at all levels.

INFORMAL SUPPORT

As one might expect, most supportive relationships at this level are found with partners, friends and relations. Most of those who had a partner (42% or nearly half the sample) found him or her supportive, but friends offered support to the majority. About a fifth of those interviewed relied on just one source of informal support. Parents mentioned friends and relatives at a great distance whom they contacted for this special support. Partners' families sometimes supplied it, even when the relationship had ended. One in 10 parents interviewed had no source of informal support (see Figure 6.2), a worrying finding given that informal support appears to be a buffer to the stress of parenting.

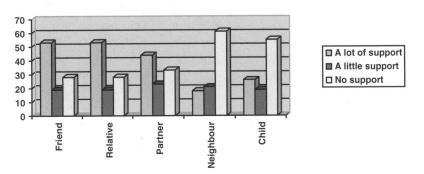

Figure 6.2   Amount and source of informal support

The extended interviews indicated that parents with informal help were better able to organize their lives and seize learning and work opportunities.

Our scoring system for levels of support is not fully developed and so associations with other measures should be seen as tentative. Informal support seems to be most important. It was the only type to relate significantly to other measures at first interview, to stress levels ($p = .000$) and to children's behaviour problems ($p = .009$). Lack of informal support was associated with higher levels of difficulty on these measures. As we have seen, informal support was also associated with positive outcomes for children in terms of attaining or maintaining a 'noncritical' score on behaviour after six months ($p = .000$). It appeared to be a relatively stable characteristic, there being a significant correlation between the measure at first and second interview ($p = .000$). It is associated with respondents' overall view of the neighbourhood ($p = .000$).

NSPCC family support projects explicitly promoted informal contacts through their open activities and group work and some specifically undertook befriending using volunteers. A function of the NSPCC project frequently mentioned by staff and service users was to reduce the isolation and stress of being alone with children and create opportunities for friendship and social and educational activity.

What Parents Said about Informal Support

At Metropolitan Outskirts project, there were several extended families on the Estate. Some carers could say, for example,

> *Most of my good friends live at a distance but I have a few nearby—my best friend is my mum and she's next door, my sister and her child is in the next road to me and my other sister and her four are round the corner.*
> Mother aged 19, with two children

Marital breakdown did not necessarily end support between families.

> *My mother and my ex-husband's mother give me a lot of support.*
> Mother aged 23, with one child

In some cases a small child offered more than adult relatives.

> *My partner and my neighbour offer me a little support, but my friend and (child under two years) are most of my support—he comes up and says 'big hug'—I would not know where to be without him.*
> Mother aged 32, with two children

> *If you are down, children perk you up, they give you something to live for.*
> Father aged 36, with one child

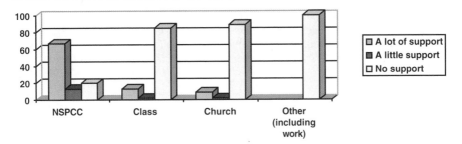

Figure 6.3 Amount and source of semi-formal support

SEMI-FORMAL SUPPORT

The semi-formal level indicated support from contacts in the community *other* than family, friends and immediate neighbours—involvement in groups, clubs and activities including work, volunteering or further education and the NSPCC or similar projects (Figure 6.3). The number of very supportive contacts per family at this level were fewer.

Over half of the respondents had only one source of *strong* support in the community beyond the informal level outside of family, friends and immediate neighbours—and this was almost always the local NSPCC project. Fourteen percent of respondents had no source of strong support at this level, but nearly all said that they received some degree of support from the project. It was the single most often quoted source of support at any level.

What Parents Said about Semi-formal Support

Where parents had a source of support other than the NSPCC in the community, for instance adult education, this had frequently come about through contact with the project. In Metropolitan Suburb, the project had strong links with a community education worker and put women in touch with English, Maths and Computer classes with crèche provision, about which they were enthusiastic. Those who mentioned further education were more likely to have a supportive family. They had often been able to organise several sources of support:

> *I keep busy and I visit people on Wednesday and Thursday; and take (two-year-old) to a playgroup twice a week for two hours and on the other three days, I come here (NSPCC Activity Groups for women) and (daughter) goes into the crèche at 25p a session. I really enjoy English and Maths classes at the local school, I started off doing maths at the NSPCC Activity Group.*
>
> Single Mother aged 24, with child aged $2\frac{1}{2}$

> *I do the counselling and art workshops here (NSPCC) and use the crèche for the two-year old. It gives you confidence doing it. I find (NSPCC worker) very approachable. Then I do a computer and maths course once a week and I get on well with the others and the tutor there. So I would say I get a lot of support in this community.*
>
> Mother aged 40, with children aged 4 and 2

A few parents mentioned religion or a specific place of worship and community activity, as a source of support outside the immediate family. The same was true of work, even where the remuneration was low:

> *I do enjoy my work—it breaks the day up. I'm a dinner lady and I love working with children. I earn £90 a month. The NSPCC is brilliant and the Church Youth Club for (son aged 13) helps me a bit.*
>
> Mother aged 46, with children aged 13 and 11

> *I supervise the cleaners at the local college, every night 5 p.m.–9.30 p.m. I walk there and someone gives me a lift home. I love it, I couldn't be without it. I might do some childminding as well. If I do I will bring the children to the (NSPCC) playgroup. NSPCC is a lot of support. You can't fault them.*
>
> Mother, with partner and three children aged 12, 7 and 3 years

> *I am a bath attendant for older people. I do that 20 hours a week for £5.66 an hour. It is decent pay and I love the work, it helps me a lot.*
>
> Mother aged 39, with three children.

Parents whose children were too old to use the NSPCC project had difficulty finding other cheap, safe activities and interests for them, and if they were able to afford transport, often travelled considerable distances to find such resources outside the local community.

Service users were most enthusiastic when they described their own personal support network at the community level, offering some routine and continuity for themselves *and* their children from week to week. This might include a class or leisure activity, work, and activities for themselves and a child or children at the NSPCC project, each week. Projects with an explicit community work and/or outreach philosophy had clear aims in this area, intending that service users move on from family support eventually and become involved with other community activities that offered them choice, but also a degree of structure and motivation.

FORMAL SUPPORT

Formal support included all professionals, including those from the health, social services, education and the police departments (Figure 6.4). Service users might have to travel some distance to access some of these. For many parents and carers, particularly those struggling with specific problems, these

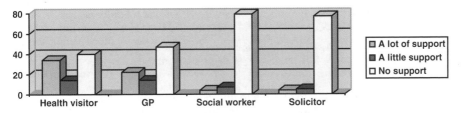

Figure 6.4 Amount and source of formal support ($N = 88$)

sources of support were as important to carers as their informal family and other close relationships. Health visitors, for instance, were quoted as often as partners in terms of instances of help and support, and GPs were seen as more supportive than neighbours.

It may be misleading to say that health visitors as a group are seen as highly supportive to parents. Rather, a *particular* health visitor in a neighbourhood (or occasionally more than one) is mentioned very frequently by name, and the same appears to be true of other professionals. The high scores for very supportive health visitors (33 mentions) actually refer to a small number of professionals, each working with several mothers. Other professionals feature much less frequently, but good (or bad) experiences had clearly made a strong impression.

Despite their importance to families under stress, well over a third of respondents could not think of one source of formal support and less than a fifth had two sources. Psychiatric and social work sources were mentioned as a previous contact by about 10% of parents.

What Parents Said about Formal Support

These quotations are from parents illustrating the level of support they received from health professionals:

> *my doctor, social worker and health visitor have all been very supportive. My children were taken off me in an emergency and they are with my mum now. The GP referred me to a clinic to get help with my drinking and the social worker lets me phone her whenever I need to. The health visitor referred me here (NSPCC) and is trying to get help for my (seven-year old) son who is all over the place. She referred him to the child consultation people. She hasn't judged me.*
>
> Mother aged 28, with children aged 7 and 2

> *There is one GP I'll wait three weeks to see.*
>
> Father aged 34, with three children

> *I went to the GP because (son) had bad eczema. He said 'you're very angry aren't you? You need to get it all out'. He was right, but I was actually there for the kids and I found that very insensitive—he could have said, 'yes the children do need this and*

I think you could do with some help too', he meant well but I did not find him supportive.
Mother aged 36, victim of domestic violence from her ex-husband, with
partner and five children

*I could only manage to take on one (of three grandchildren). So the others have been
adopted. They (Social Services) broke their promises—they said we would see the
children but we haven't. We have met the adoptive parents now, that helped. They don't
come to see him and they don't pay us. They should show more interest if you're fostering.*
Grandfather aged 62, with grandson aged 12 on Residence Order

As discussed in Chapter 3, some of the women with the most serious health
problems appeared to have received inadequate support:

*I have sickle cell and am often depressed and in pain. The Sickle Cell Unit does offer
some support, for example they referred me to Social Services for help with the children.
But when I am admitted in a crisis I am often in hospital for weeks on end and I'm put
with women with cancer. My friends bring the children in to cheer me up and of course
it doesn't work well.*
Mother aged 34, with three children

*I'm deaf in one ear and the Audiology department said 'you know this is progressive,
don't you'? And nothing else. I need to know how bad it is—will my hearing go
completely? In case I need more help. The hearing aids they supply crackle all the
time—they are not very good. They don't seem to care.*
Mother aged 30, with one child

If we take all levels of support—informal (family, immediate neighbours,
and friends), semi-formal (community) and formal (professional), we find
that half of the parents and carers (50%) have a supportive relationship
at each level (Figure 6.5). A third (33%) have a very supportive relationship at two out of three levels, informal plus semi-formal being the most
common.

Several areas for exploration are suggested by these data. We can begin to
plot and to compare a profile for the 'social capital' of different groups. For
instance, it would be interesting to compare the 'networks' and 'community
climate' scores of parents using family support in the community with a
comparison group relying on informal networks only.

The profile of support appears to vary between the user-groups from project
to project. In some there are higher levels of informal support and formal, professional help seems to be more accessible. With a larger population we could
perhaps begin to compare neighbourhoods as having a different 'climate'.
They seem to vary from *warm*, with support being available from a variety of
sources and levels, and there is a real 'fabric' of support networks, through
cool, where one or more levels is weaker and patchier, to *cold*, where respondents maintain any supportive contact with difficulty. For our respondents,
there appeared to be some key elements in 'community climate':

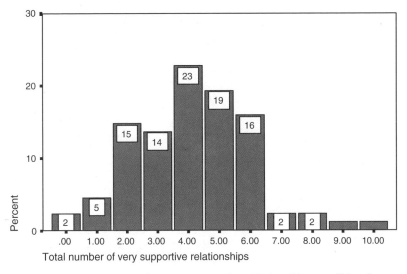

Figure 6.5   Amount of strong supportive relationships, at all levels

- positive support from close friends and family, who need not live locally
- housing policy, achieving consistency and desirability of tenure, related to residents' commitment to the locality
- good quality and community outreach by agencies, particularly primary healthcare, schools, further education, police, with back up from specialist agencies such as social services and mental health services
- involvement of local people with community development agencies, including family support
- for young people, the degree of isolation and insecurity they experience in the community, their degree of trust in key adults, and the number of safe constructive activities in which they can engage, are measures of the hostility or otherwise of the local community climate

SUMMARY: CARERS' SUPPORT NETWORKS

- The majority of supportive relationships were informal, i.e. with partners, relatives and friends. Friends were the most common source of strong support. Parents took trouble in order to obtain personal support, keeping in touch with relatives at a great distance or with an ex-partner's family. Using a tentative scoring system, we find this level of support to be associated with other measures used in the study, that is, measures of stress, children's behavioural difficulties and community climate.

- 10% of respondents had no source of strong informal support.
- At the semi-formal or community level, the local NSPCC projects were by far the most commonly mentioned source of support, by over 80% of respondents. A few mentioned work, adult education or religious affiliation as very supportive. Work, even if poorly paid, was highly valued in this way. Nearly a sixth of respondents had no source of strong support in their community.
- Over a third of respondents had no professional or formal support. Health visitors were most often quoted as very supportive but closer examination suggests that a small number of professionals were the source of the most positive statements. A minority had experienced an insensitive or negative response from professionals, increasing their isolation.
- Taking respondents' estimate of the local area as well as their levels of support we can plot the local 'community climate'. Factors identified in other studies are high levels of risk to children, social impoverishment and the failure of support systems. Themes that came up in our respondents' view of 'community climate' were levels of personal support and safety (also mentioned by children), housing policy, and accessibility of the key agencies, particularly health and mental health services and social services.
- With a caveat about the preliminary nature of our scoring support networks, we found significant associations between parents' level of informal support, and whether children attained or maintained behaviour that gave less concern.

7

OVERVIEW OF FAMILY SUPPORT PROVIDED BY THE NSPCC

This section of the book provides the wider context of family support services used by the families we have already described. In this chapter, we look at the history of family support in the NSPCC, and at the results of a survey of all the NSPCC's projects, undertaken for the study. This includes the range and distribution of their family support services, aims, funding arrangements and the mix of staff skills.

In Chapter 8, detailed examples have been taken from projects whose service users (parents, carers, children) and staff were interviewed for the research. The examples concern the history and day-to-day practice of the projects, with comments from interviewees about the service and the local neighbourhood. In Chapter 9, we look at the bigger picture of local authority services for children and families, and how they measure up in terms of the government's Quality Protects Initiative and other audit material. Implications for the development of family support practice are drawn out at the end of each chapter.

In 1999, NSPCC had 140 active projects across Northern Ireland, Wales and England. Some were one-person projects and some large enough to run miniprojects of their own. They were all sent a questionnaire about family support and about a third of them replied. This data was supplemented by NSPCC's management data and information provided at staff seminars, and forms the evidence for this chapter. Since the survey, NSPCC services have been reorganised but the data and issues raised remain highly relevant.

RANGE AND DEPTH OF FAMILY SUPPORT WORK

Thirty projects (some 20% of all projects) replied that they had a major family support function, as defined in Section 17 Part III of the Children Act

1989—'services intended to safeguard and promote the welfare of children in need and so far as is consistent with that duty, to promote the upbringing of such children by their families'. A further 30 projects said that their primary activity was with children in need of protection. They had an underlying role that they identified as supporting families and promoting social inclusion. Examples were 'empowering parents by advocating for better local services', 'improving access to local services for children and families' or 'improving community networks'.

During reorganisation of NSPCC's work into four programmes in 1999–2000, the Family Support and Quality Parenting Programme included approximately 55 projects with £9.4 million NSPCC funding. The boundaries of the programmes and their relative size have changed over the two-year period of the research. Before reorganisation, the number and size of projects in each of NSPCC's seven geographical regions also differed greatly (Figure 7.1), in response to the pattern of services locally and funding partners' expectations. The NSPCC is currently aiming for a more consistent distribution of services across the country, and this means staff changing the services they offer. Skills profiling and retraining will be crucial to the success of these shifts in service priorities.

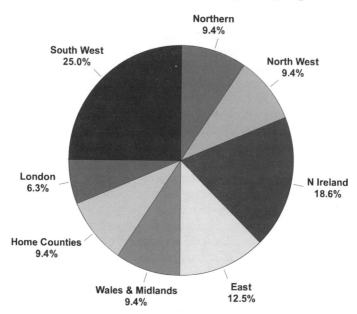

Distribution of family support projects by region

Figure 7.1   Distribution of NSPCC family support projects by region

WHY UNDERTAKE FAMILY SUPPORT?

Projects with a major family support function were asked for their statement of purpose or mission. These included *promotion of children's welfare* as often as *prevention or treatment of harm*. Projects more often saw these two aims (promotion and prevention) as interrelated than the highly specialised image of NSPCC would suggest. For instance a fifth of the projects declaring a family support function were child protection teams. To complement and follow up therapeutic work and specialised counselling, they offer advocacy to help families obtain other services, and practical help including toys, equipment and holidays.

Project workers in these teams made comments such as:

> using skills in joint interviewing with the police we may help to bring an abuser to court, but sometimes it is helpful to get a change of housing or a holiday which sustains the family through months or years of waiting for the outcome of a prosecution; or to help to sort out a child's disrupted education.

> It is not always possible just to plonk a child protection service down in the middle of a community. If we start off finding out what is wanted locally and providing it, we can make a better fit with local people and services.

Many NSPCC practitioners had developed strongly child-centred work while including parents as partners and, in some cases, as co-workers. They questioned whether a one-dimensional image of children as *only* or predominately, weak, vulnerable and victimised may not disadvantage them further. They commented that identifying strengths or protective factors such as children's ability to develop *confidence* alongside *caution*, may instead be a key to achieving NSPCC's vision of eradicating child abuse by 2020. To empower children (for instance, so that their views on services are heard directly), without them becoming unappealing, or even threatening, is a challenging shift of perception for our society and for the NSPCC as a key definer of attitudes in this area.

Practitioners also suggested that work on stress-inducing matters, such as finances, health and adult relationships, is often essential if parents are to take advantage of work directed at improving their ability to listen to and negotiate with their children without boiling over. The same is true of the need to deal with children's stress from educational, familial or peer pressures, while they learn to express their views without destructive or self-harming behaviour. In other words, practitioners thought that many instances of harm arise from a number of interacting sources of vulnerability and stress, and prevention thus means making available a range of interacting types of family support.

WHO IS OFFERED FAMILY SUPPORT?

For these reasons, and others, most projects that responded had strong elements of family support, including advocacy, advice and practical help. Those with a major family support role tended to prioritise work, firstly with parents of pre-school children, who were offered activities with a crèche or structured play for the child, and secondly with parents of school-age children already identified as vulnerable by parents or professionals.

Parents of pre-school children were divided evenly between those who self-referred and referrals by a health visitor, while parents of the older age group tended to be referred. However, a substantial proportion, at least one third, came because of personal recommendation. Often the project put parents in touch with one another and so they began to form an informal support network before they first came to the project (see Chapter 6).

It is attractive for projects to focus preventative services on pre-school children with evident difficulties, because services are easier to organise, and problems appear to resolve more quickly at this age (see Chapter 4). However, there are several difficulties with this approach. Firstly, the research offers some evidence that where the majority of children receiving the service have severe behavioural difficulties, positive outcomes—at least in short to medium term—are fewer, whereas there are many more positive outcomes for children with difficulties where these children are in the minority. This suggests a 'cumulative' effect of non-problem or problem behaviour. In other words, focusing resources exclusively on 'problematic' behaviour not only raises issues of labelling, but may reduce the effectiveness of a service.

Secondly, parents who bring pre-school children to projects frequently do so to prevent the development in their younger children of problems they were already experiencing with school-age children and about whom they also sought advice. Projects whose activities and skills were tuned to early years were adapting these approaches to demands for advice with older children.

Thirdly, even if local services for school-age children with behavioural difficulties were to improve, the baseline appears so poor that it is most unlikely that this demand would abate. In terms of preventing significant harm to children, while there are proportionally more registrations of very young children as at risk, similar numbers of children aged 1–4 and 5–9 are being registered annually. Of children starting to be looked after, nearly one third (31%), the highest proportion, are separated from their families because of actual or apprehended harm and a further 20% because of behaviour including risk of offending (Department of Health, 2001).

COSTING SERVICES

Unit costing for preventative family services is still woefully underdeveloped in this country. The Department of Health has been struggling with unit costing for services for children in need for several years, producing guidance recently (Department of Health, 2000b). Our rough estimates for NSPCC's services suggest that some 1,500 families may receive a 'structured family service' (e.g., a parent training course) and a further 3,000 families less formal advice and support each year. Taking the global figure of £9.5 million for the NSPCC's Quality Parenting and Family Support Programmes would give an estimated average cost of approximately £40 per family per week for preventive family support services (including all members receiving a service from a one off-visit to lengthy counselling, all overheads, etc). While effectiveness remains to be fully demonstrated, on the basis of limited financial data the services appear to be economical at least. Contact time is high in these services, most families receiving between one and six hours of activities per week.

Family support services need much more detailed costing to identify hidden costs and seasonal variations. It appears that unit costs vary widely from project to project and from year to year. This may depend on efficiency, but also on factors such as cost of premises and of temporary staffing cover, which are not easily controlled.

FUNDING SOURCES AND PARTNERSHIPS

The majority of funding came from the NSPCC, its source being charitable giving by individuals and institutions. The proportion of such funding varied by project from 100% to under 30%. The range of project budgets was extremely wide, from under £10K to over £2 million per year, and the amount of partnership funding varied accordingly.

Among the survey respondents, there were three main groups of partnerships in descending order of frequency: with local public services, with voluntary and private agencies, and with other national voluntary organisations. Over 50% had partnerships with local authority, social services or education departments and nearly a third with health trusts or (in Northern Ireland) Health and Social Services Boards (Figure 7.2). The remaining partnerships were with a variety of local agencies: housing associations, local voluntary organisations and businesses. Very occasionally there was a partnership arrangement with another national voluntary organisation where the two could provide complementary but distinguishable services. Partners provided both direct funding and/or resources such as buildings or skills, for example, sessions from an educational psychologist. Projects faced year-on-year

Funding partners for family support services

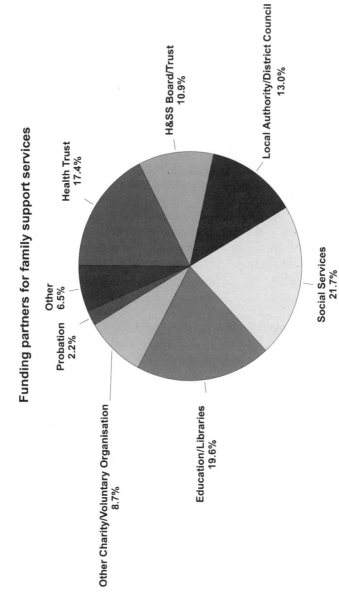

H&SS Board/Trust
10.9%

Local Authority/District Council
13.0%

Health Trust
17.4%

Social Services
21.7%

Other
6.5%

Probation
2.2%

Education/Libraries
19.6%

Other Charity/Voluntary Organisation
8.7%

Figure 7.2   Funding partners for family support services

funding reviews by local authorities, which, in many areas, presented the threat of loss of services or staff and much-needed continuity for families (see Chapters 5 and 8). Depending on management priorities, a shortfall in funding might be cushioned by the NSPCC, but this was by no means certain.

INPUT: SKILLS MIX AND DISTRIBUTION

The skills mix in family support work in NSPCC appeared to be very diverse. Projects with a major family support role employed qualified social workers as the largest staff grouping, closely followed by nursery nursing, backed up by staff with play therapy and pre-school practice diplomas. Nursing, midwifery and health visiting formed a third grouping and there was a scattering of community work, business, management and administrative qualifications and various other degrees. Some staff members had several qualifications. (See Figure 7.3: this figure does not show very small groups.)

The qualifications and the experience they represent are an extremely valuable toolbox for developing high quality family support. There are technical and practical skills in work with all age groups of children and a very broad range of developmental problems. Just as many projects offering mainly child protection also have family support services, so too can the latter projects often draw on social work skills to support children and families through an investigation and/or the prosecution of an abuser.

There is a scattering of strong research, community work and/or business and entrepreneurial skills either brought to the project or learnt on the job, but staff say that they need better access to research and data-processing skills.

Family support staff are distributed thinly. The average number per project was 2.5, with many projects having just one staff member. The staff to service user ratio, estimated on the figures quoted above as 1:56 families, appears very cost-effective. The downside is the cost of management support to isolated staff and the risk of activities shutting down with the illness or departure of a single individual. Reorganisation has been aimed at ensuring the viability of projects.

CONTENT, METHODS AND LOCATION OF FAMILY SUPPORT SERVICES

Evidence for this section was gathered from the survey and the more detailed information supplied by projects directly involved in the research. Projects with a major family support function typically offer a menu or spectrum of services. These include community events open to the public, holiday play

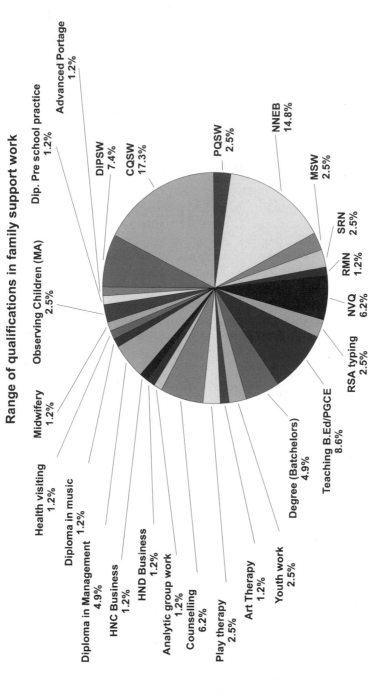

Figure 7.3 Range of qualifications in NSPCC's family support work (MA, Master of Arts; Dipsw, Diploma in Social Work; CQSW, Certificate of Qualification in Social Work; PQSW, Post Qualifying Social Work Training; PGCE, Post Graduate Certificate in Education; NNEB, National Nursing Examining Board; MSW, Medical Social Worker; SRN, State Registered Nurse; RMN, Registered Mental Nurse; NVQ, National Vocational Qualification; RSA, Royal Society of Arts; BEd, Bachelor of Education; HND, Higher National Diploma; HNC, Higher National Certificate)

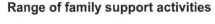

Range of family support activities

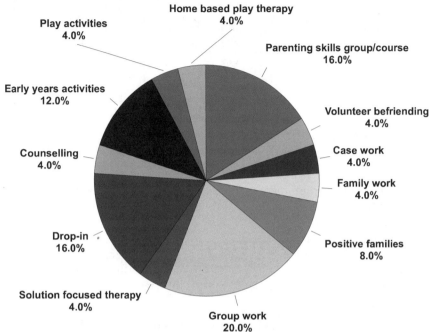

Figure 7.4   Range of family support activities

activities, outings and events to which service users may bring family and friends, and a drop-in held once or twice each week with a crèche for younger children and possibly play activities for older pre-school children (Figure 7.4). It is a major achievement that these services are maintained consistently week after week, often by the same small staff group that provided the more intensive services. Parents and volunteers assisted, but NSPCC staff members were never out of reach.

Other services include one-off or occasional advice and advocacy; counselling, group work, group therapy; skills development or parenting training sessions; and volunteer visiting. Projects were experimenting with techniques based on behavioural psychology, such as video home guidance. Many of the services are developed with reference to local or national university-based research commissioned for the purpose, and the majority of services are evaluated after each session or series of sessions. However, the use of follow-up and comparison groups is rare.

Where NSPCC ran a family centre, most of the services were based there, with some visiting undertaken to the family home. Half the projects involved in the research had an office base only and ran their services in community centres, health centres and schools.

Work in and with groups is highly developed, characterising over two thirds of the family support services. Groups were often difficult to establish, particularly with new target populations but, once up and running, took on their own momentum and appeared to be very cost-effective, promoting mutual support and informal networks. The difficulty in long-established groups was to broaden and diversify their membership and activities, and to call 'time' on service users who no longer needed or contributed much to the work.

All the projects undertook some strategic work. This included representation on bodies influencing local policy on services for children and families. Some projects were also very active in terms of the local community, for instance hosting meetings and undertaking surveys, in order to raise awareness on matters of child and family welfare.

STAFF VIEWS: STRENGTHS, WEAKNESSES, OPPORTUNITIES AND THREATS

Evidence was drawn from the survey and analyses of strengths, weaknesses, opportunities and threats undertaken by the research projects. Staff involved in family support and their managers in the NSPCC are in general, without being naïve, refreshingly enthusiastic; firstly about the potential children and families have to change, even in adverse circumstances, and also about the services they are providing and the teams they work in. They enjoyed the informal aspect of the work, for instance, the fun and camaraderie between staff and parents that went into setting up a group. But this did not detract from the seriousness with which they sought to address poor or harmful parenting, to learn from evaluation or to keep in touch with new practice developments.

They said that the positive elements in family support, which kept them energised and prevented burn-out, were

- seeing evidence of recovery, for example, a parent who had hurt a child learning to discipline without physical punishment, and to enjoy the child's company more; a child's name either removed from the child protection register, or not needing to join it
- obtaining positive feedback from parents, children and referrers; cards and letters of thanks adorn many desks
- the status of the organisation. The NSPCC generally has a reputation for a high standard of work
- support in terms of supervision, training and guidance, especially concerning harm to children

Most NSPCC family support workers show confidence and a degree of openness to evaluation, even where this is critical, which makes learning and service development a positive challenge. Well over a third of family support staff surveyed had improved their skills and qualifications while staying with NSPCC.

Nevertheless, the view of many staff was that the organisation remained undecided overall about the value of family support, resulting in mixed messages. They thought the status and pay of family support workers was relatively low and relevant training difficult to obtain and/or expensive. They thought that NSPCC's advertising encouraged a one-dimensional view of family problems.

Staff also saw external changes, which might provide opportunities or threats. Among others, the following practice issues were thought relevant:

Central government initiatives such as Quality Protects, On Track, Connexions and Sure Start have changed the pattern of service provision.

Local authority social services for children have been focussed on improving outcomes for children already in the child protection or children looked after systems.

Children in need are (correctly or otherwise) perceived as a lesser priority, and local authorities often have just two or three 'showcase' projects working with very small relative numbers.

Services such as Sure Start give intensive coverage but over relatively small areas and for younger age groups. Like many organisations, the NSPCC has to consider whether such initiatives fit with its goals and the most effective locations for its services.

The organisation's relationship with the statutory sector can be a complex one. The NSPCC gains from its clear profile as a child rescue organisation; it is easily recognised, and donors understand why they are giving their money. The NSPCC undertakes a great deal of awareness-raising and also highly specialised work investigating paedophilia, identifying dangerous repeat abusers, working with young abusers, and assisting children and non-abusing parents to recover from abuse and achieve a prosecution, if not always the conviction, of the offender. However, most child protection work is undertaken by democratically accountable local authority social services, to the tune of at least 120,000 preliminary child protection investigations a year (Department of Health, 2001). The NSPCC rightly defends its independence to criticise local authorities' practice. For local authorities the NSPCC is a valuable source of specialist expertise; it also has legal child protection powers it now rarely uses, without a legal obligation to meet unremitting local needs to ever-higher standards. The NSPCC has the authority to challenge the weaknesses of current childcare systems but, if it does so, has to take on the ensuing controversy about resources and the relatively huge numbers dealt with by the statutory sector. Local NSPCC staff in partnership arrangements with a local authority have to steer the relationship through the various political currents of the two organisations.

The NSPCC has to decide whether to specialise yet further, for instance in combating child exploitation via the Internet. It also has to decide whether to develop its early intervention and preventive work as well and if so, in what proportions and particularly in what partnerships. In many families coming to the NSPCC for preventive support, an adult had suffered violence or abuse, but neglect or non-accidental injury to a child had either not occurred or was being actively addressed. Parents did not see themselves as 'perpetrators' and children were not, or were no longer, 'victims'. To publicise this work is not easy; it complicates the NSPCC's traditionally clear-cut image. However, it may be essential in order to identify and promote the strengths in children, families and wider networks of support that can survive and put an end to a cycle of abuse. This in turn may lead to better understanding of the tragic cases in which this has not proved possible.

SUMMARY

- In response to paper and telephone surveys, nearly half of NSPCC's 140 projects said that they had a primary or secondary family support role as defined in the Children Act 1989, i.e. safeguarding and promoting the welfare of children in need, so far as possible, within their own families.
- Half of these projects were primarily working with children who had been physically or sexually abused. They used family support to sustain and improve the quality of life for family members, on the basis that, in their view, this improved the likelihood of a good recovery.
- Areas of work for other projects were domestic violence; emotional harm and/or neglect; family stress with children out of control.
- Variety characterised family support; variety of partner agencies, skills and activities. The most common partnership arrangements were with local public social services, education and health; local voluntary and community organisations; and regionally with other national voluntary organisations. About a quarter of staff had a social work qualification; others had nursery nursing, teaching and a range of health qualifications.
- Methods of work included many forms of group work, informal and structured play activities, and parenting and skills classes for adults. New methods, such as video home training, were being piloted and tested. Some of the key aims were to improve family communications; reduce stress and instances of harmful discipline; provide opportunities for good family experiences, for

example, play, outings. Most of this work was evaluated in terms of service users' satisfaction, and some of it for child development outcomes. Work with couples, whole families and with fathers was underdeveloped.

- The morale of staff was generally good in terms of confidence in their own and the organisation's standards. There was a core of staff interested in individual and organisational learning. Many staff members were concerned about the level of understanding and status of family support in the organisation and what they saw as one-dimensional portrayal of family problems in its advertising.
- Having made decisions about the focus of its practice, the NSPCC needs to sustain this in enduring partnerships with other agencies, in order to maintain consistency for families and staff and to allow meaningful follow-up evaluation and learning.

8

EXAMPLES OF FAMILY
SUPPORT PRACTICE

In this chapter, we first summarise background data on employment, housing, health and education in six localities where we researched the NSPCC's projects. We then give more detailed accounts of three of these projects, to demonstrate their differences and similarities, illustrating how they developed in their current form and the activities they provide, and including the views of children, their parents and local agency staff. In Chapter 9 we profile the wider group of children in need, including children in need of protection, in these six local authorities.

Six NSPCC projects, whose work was entirely or mainly family support, were selected as sites for intensive research. Each provided a broadly similar range of services but had evolved to meet local needs, with unique features (see Table 8.1). This is true of the NSPCC's family support as a whole (see previous chapter). The six projects identified children, parents and local family support providers who might be willing to be interviewed (for a small fee in the case of service users), and the researcher then wrote to them all. All the projects are located in, or are at the edge of, neighbourhoods that are struggling in relation to the surrounding areas. Taken together, they illustrate important issues for children and families living in adverse circumstances in the United Kingdom.

The aim is to give a picture of the social setting and quality of life for families who use the projects. In this sense the research takes an ecological perspective, insofar as this 'tries to take account of the web of interacting factors influencing individuals, groups, communities (and) can inform planned interventions at different levels whilst recognising their interconnections' (Baldwin, 2000). More recently, social exclusion has been analysed in a similar way: 'the community is influenced not only by . . . national and global influences, but also by the families and individuals who constitute it. This may seem obvious but it contrasts with much existing analysis that treats personal, family and community influences as essentially separate factors with their independent

Table 8.1 Similarities and differences in service provision

	Met S	Met O	New E	Sea S	Inner C	Garden C
Drop-in	X	✓	✓	✓	✓	✓
Childcare	✓	✓	✓	✓	✓	✓
Twice a week or more	✓	✓	✓	✓	✓	✓
One-to-one counselling	✓	✓	✓	✓	✓	✓
Social worker	X	✓	✓	✓	✓	✓
Group work for adults	X	✓	X	X	X	X
Group work for children	X	✓	X	X	✓	✓
Skills (nonparenting)	✓	✓	X	X	✓	✓
Parenting training	✓	✓	✓	✓	X	✓

effects' (Hills *et al.*, 2002). This is the context for findings about the needs of individual children and families, and about the extent to which family support can be seen to address those needs.

To maintain the confidentiality of the families we interviewed, the six projects have been given substitute names, sometimes abbreviated in the text. They are:

- *Metropolitan Suburb (Met S)*. The project is run from the top floor of a council house (above a council run playgroup) on a 1950s estate in the West Midlands. Family support services are provided on other premises.
- *Metropolitan Outskirts (Met O)*. This project operates from a three bedroom terraced council house on a pre-war estate at the edge of a town in the Northwest of England. Some services are provided on other premises.
- *New Estate (New E)*. This is a purpose-built Family Centre on an estate built by the Greater London Council in the 1960s near a large county town in the South East.
- *Sea Side (Sea S)*. This project is based at the offices of the local NSPCC Child Protection Team in a shire county town. Its services are, like Metropolitan Suburb's, provided on other premises.
- *Inner City (Inner C)*. This is also a Family Centre, located in a large Victorian house in a mixed housing area within an inner London borough.
- *Garden City (Garden C)*. The project is in a Family Centre occupying two adjacent council houses on a London overspill estate at the edge of a town in the East Midlands.

These six local authorities, where NSPCC research sites were located, all had a small proportion of wards and localities within other wards, where family needs were measurably higher than the authority's average. The NSPCC projects were in (or on the borders of) these localities. The measures used included the DfEE's Index of Local Deprivation, the Jarman (health) Index, proportion of income support claimants and youth and adult unemployment. Two out of the six authorities had combined this data with other indices of need, such as numbers of children accommodated, numbers on the child protection register and number of young offenders. They found a strong correlation between the two sets of data. Specific areas have suffered in terms of lack of investment in public housing, loss of employment and lack of transport infrastructure. The areas of high family need are often ones where there is a high concentration of families from ethnic minorities and asylum-seekers, although these families are also scattered throughout the authorities.

The six authorities differ widely in terms of the quality and availability of data. Some say they are concerned about identifying high need areas, in case doing so contributes to possible stigmatisation. There are also political sensitivities about distribution of resources across wards. Despite these constraints, one authority (Metropolitan Outskirts) had developed data collection on need sufficiently to contribute to the Department of Health database for a national survey (Department of Health, 2001).

Professionals and parents who were interviewed described very local patterns of social discrimination. For instance, in Garden City, the fact that a small shopping precinct was used for drug trafficking had caused local householders to believe they had been criminalised, and to want to move. In New Estate, the local primary school served both public and private housing but, despite its success, many parents did not want their children to 'mix with those from the estate'. Parents feared the stigma of identifying with a 'difficult' area, and this paralysed efforts to improve the situation. For parents, the bottom line was to have the support of your family and, if possible, work. Without either you were in trouble, and living in an area you hated compounded the difficulty. While a positive view of the local community did not necessarily solve personal problems, it gave the chance of developing a personal and social network and, in some cases, motivation to improve the neighbourhood. Outreach to isolated parents, and children, in the form of a bridge or substitute network (see Chapter 5) was thus crucial to community development, and (our findings suggest) over time, to parents' stress levels and to their assessment of children's behaviour.

METROPOLITAN SUBURB

The estate where the NSPCC project is located is on the outskirts of a West Midlands City.

The decline of local industry speeded up in the recession of the late 1980s. The economic infrastructure to what were largely working class council estates—shops, public houses, post offices, leisure—had been stripped away along with employment.

In a city ranked in the 25% most deprived local authorities in England (Index of Local Deprivation, 1998), deprivation in this suburb is almost twice that of the city average. The three local wards include one where 37.7% of children are in low or non-earning households (city average is 25%) and where 12.3% of children are in unsuitable accommodation (city average is 6.8%).

Earnings and involvement in higher education are both below the city average. Health indicators are equally a cause for serious concern. This part of the city has the highest birth rate for teenage women (756 per 10,000 as against 299 per 10,000 for the city) and the second highest rate for underweight births. Other health data suggest the devastating cumulative effects of stress and poverty on families. The mortality rate for males aged 45–64 is over two and a half times the city average at 78 per 10,000 and suicide rates are very high (Health Trust data).

Using measures of the population of under 18, children of lone parents and children receiving free school meals, the ward in which the NSPCC project is located is one of the four most deprived in the city, and at the time of this study (1998–2001) there were real signs of social disintegration.

Comments about Metropolitan Suburb

The quality of life can vary from very bad to quite good, depending on the specific street or close you live in. If you have extended family, if you get help when you need it, that makes a big difference—people struggle with parenting otherwise.

NSPCC Worker

I have moved out and I still come back to the community centre for the activities and crèche—they are the best around.

Parent

Where I live is just across the brook but there is a field in front of the houses so you see the children playing. Here it is really dangerous with the turning off each street and the cars driving so fast. A little girl was playing in a parking area and a car backed into her and killed her and it is not the first time. She was only three years old.

Parent

The lack of play space and shops is a problem. The goods are poor and expensive, because there is no local competition. People are terrified of drug users—cannabis, heroin, prescribed methadone. I've heard that families moving in have been 'visited' and told what will happen if they report anything. And some having to move out under escort because they did report.

Health Visitor

It's exactly what I was told about before I moved here. You see youths break into empty homes, damage cars, siphon off petrol. The house next to me is empty and the fire brigade have been in twice—I'm terrified of a fire there. People know who is responsible but they don't inform because of repercussions. They made a few arrests and there were demonstrations on the street—I think the police decided to keep a low profile.

Parent

> *Other people think it's your fault, and that you are happy living as you are and don't want to improve your life or the lives of your children. We are caught in a trap we can't get out of, though you do learn to survive. But we don't just want to survive, we have standards too. We want a nice home and to have a clean tidy estate instead of looking out on piles of rubbish.*
>
> Parent quoted in Baldwin and Curruthers, 1998

Providers of children's services for Metropolitan Suburb draw attention to the corrosive effect of poverty, not only on family life, but also on the very services designed to mitigate its effects. In their view, pressure on local services comes, not only through local need, but also through national policy:

> Central government has increasingly influenced local services by imposing additional responsibilities but tightly restricting additional resources to pay for them . . . some work can no longer be carried out and many needs cannot be met by the statutory authorities. It is our difficult task to decide which needs take priority. (Joint Health/Social Services Plan for Metropolitan Outskirts, 1997–2000)

However, they admit that services are inconsistent because 'there is no integrated strategic planning for family support across the whole city'.

How the Project was Set Up

In the absence of such a strategy, agencies in specific areas of the city have developed their own approaches. In Metropolitan Suburb, where the NSPCC project is located, community development methods are used. Child protection registration has been high in the suburb and social services overwhelmed by demands for intervention (see Chapter 9). Local parents were very concerned about child safety on the estate and that referral for child protection was the only route to a service. It was thought important to listen to these complaints and enable local people to share more responsibility and control over the use of what resources there were for preventive work.

In the 1990s, a handful of NSPCC workers in Metropolitan Suburb were engaged in community development, action research and service delivery, in equal proportions. Rather than one survey or pilot study followed by a single funding process, there have been numerous smaller studies in partnership with various local groups and agencies. This process has meant an investment of time and funding in work on the joint local strategy, in parallel with direct work with families. It could be argued that this diverts from helping children in need. However, project workers and other local staff thought that the involvement of families in research and planning led to services with greater impact relative to resources, because they were more relevant to local needs. Certainly it was the only project we studied, other than those

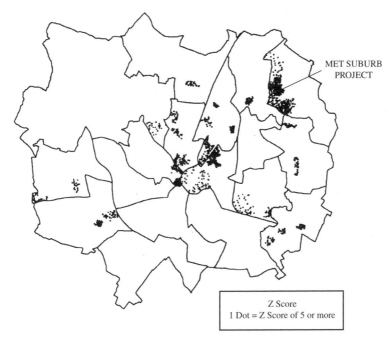

MET SUBURB
PROJECT

Z Score
1 Dot = Z Score of 5 or more

Figure 8.1 Map showing areas of city falling into the most disadvantaged 10%
for the (West Midlands) region.
Source: Baldwin and Curruthers (1998). Reproduced with permission from *Developing
Neighbourhood Support and Child Protection Strategies* © Ashgate Publishing Limited.

specifically aimed at Black families, which had succeeded in providing services to a cross-section of local communities.

The project's action research and strategic activity includes surveys of access to childcare and adult education opportunities for Black and ethnic minority families; work to build a family support strategy for the city; and research into child safety in the project area, involving parents, workers and academics. A wide range of service developments has followed, some of which are described below. For a fuller account of the rationale for the project's work the reader is referred to Baldwin and Curruthers (1998). Two maps have been reproduced from that work, showing firstly, areas of deprivation (Figure 8.1) and secondly, levels of child protection registration in the city (Figure 8.2). There is an apparent relationship between the two, particularly in the northwest area where Met Suburb project was set up. Tables 8.2 and 8.3 show service users' view of a range of family support projects across the city.

The project manager saw this approach to meeting the needs of children and families as partly the result of community development, as opposed to social

Number of children on protection register
in different wards of city

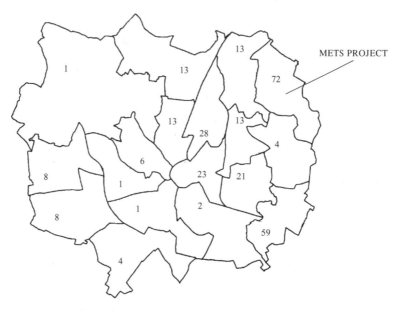

Figure 8.2 Map of city showing March 1989 registrations.
Source: Baldwin and Curruthers (1998). Reproduced with permission from *Developing Neighbourhood Support and Child Protection Strategies* © Ashgate Publishing Limited.

work, training. Certainly local professionals found her approach energising in an area where unremitting work on individual cases could leave professionals exhausted or cynical:

> she is prepared to ask the uncomfortable questions and is very clear—the excellence of the project is that it has developed services with others and in response to the changing needs of this area. (Education Worker)

Some of the key aims of the Metropolitan Suburb project are:

- to work with parents to define their own needs and problems in bringing up children, and to identify resources needed and parents' preferred solutions
- to improve the sensitivity and effectiveness of local services for children and families, through collaborative work
- to help parents provide written accounts of their experience that can be used in training professionals
- to identify and promote preventive initiatives to reduce child protection concerns
- to demonstrate the usefulness of self-help and family-support programmes as a major priority in child protection.

Table 8.2   Use of local childcare services (131 respondents)

Resource (no. using resource)	Comments of those interviewed
Baby clinic (103)	55 – met children's needs 55 – held at convenient times 8 – sometimes had long wait Staff told them 'how to do it' Not always open when needed milk
Nursery (86)	Too expensive No places for children below normal age range More provision needed for children to stay all day
Parents and toddlers groups (48)	At inconvenient times Didn't know where to find Hard to get involved
Playgroups (53)	Expensive Not enough places
Babysitters (28)	No one to ask Unsure who could be trusted
Crèches (27)	Don't know where to find Staff aren't always qualified Children not always happy there Too far away Too expensive
Holiday playschemes (26)	Opening hours inconvenient Expensive
Childminders (10)	Too expensive
After school care (1)	Unaware of any provision

Source: Baldwin and Curruthers (1998). Reproduced with permission from *Developing Neighbourhood Support and Child Protection Strategies* © Ashgate Publishing Limited.

In other words, the views of service users, and evidence of service effectiveness, have been equally important in trying to achieve best practice in preventive work. These principles are now built into the Best Value framework for local authority services. Clearly, parents who had been consulted thought the approach had made a difference. Parents quoted by Baldwin and Curruthers said:

we have the same fears as professionals have for our children—we also have the same expectations for them as everyone else does. We have found that people do care about our children, but we need support to carry on caring.

We all have a responsibility to keep children safe. Since we began talking to policy makers, attitudes about parents living on this estate have changed. Two years ago we were told that it would be impossible to have a safe play area on the estate. Now the local authority has identified £200,000 to build one, in consultation with local parents and children. The

Table 8.3   Use of local services for Black children (66 respondents)

Resource (no. using resource)	Comments of those interviewed
Baby clinic (37)	21 – met children's needs 20 – held at convenient times 2 – had language problems 1 – no welcome for Black people 1 – times not convenient
Nursery (40)	11 – met children's needs Prefer longer hours Access was restrictive
Parents and toddlers groups (8)	4 – met children's needs Not used by African Caribbean parents or parents of children of mixed African Caribbean heritage Child wouldn't go Expensive Time wasting None in area Lack of information
Playgroups (16)	Not long enough hours Too far away
Babysitters (5)	No comment
Crèches (7)	Too expensive Unsure where to find
Holiday playschemes (3)	No comment
Childminders (3)	Too expensive 1 – difficulty finding minder for disabled child
After school care (3)	No comment

Source: Baldwin and Curruthers (1998). Reproduced with permission from *Developing Neighbourhood Support and Child Protection Strategies* © Ashgate Publishing Limited.

> *local authority has also shown a commitment to providing childcare and to ensure that their meetings are scheduled at times that parents can attend. The NSPCC has responded positively to our views by providing our area with co-ordination and administration time for the project ... and providing support to local parents, particularly those more likely to be isolated, through a network of trained 'parent volunteers'.*

It is of interest that the NSPCC project is registered as a charity in its own right so that it can fund-raise for itself. The project budget is now £132,000 per annum. It is delivered from an office base, and uses local community centre premises to run groups and to provide childcare, primarily for parents of pre-school-age children. Other groups and crèches are run on nearby estates from church halls or health centres. There are just three staff: a full-time volunteer co-ordinator, who is an ex-teacher, a part-time (nursery nurse trained) childcare co-ordinator and a family support development worker who is a graduate.

Project Services

The project has combined professional knowledge, particularly in the fields of community development, adult education and child protection, to great effect by recruiting and training volunteers direct from the community to assist families. The benefits are multiple:

- the service is the result of a full and open consultation—it is therefore well known already and has a positive reputation
- for most parents, there is less stigma in a befriending service than in professionals visiting
- the project had a more diverse group of service users and volunteers than others, as a result of its surveys and outreach services
- the volunteers benefit from training and work experience and some go on to paid employment
- although volunteers are not a cheap option, there is cost saving in some cases—the cost of training volunteers and support to families was offset by savings on crisis services, which in some cases were the only alternative.

The infrastructure that makes this scheme work is carefully planned and every volunteer is provided with a Volunteer Pack, a job description, person specification, self-assessment, police checks, training and regular supervision. Other services run by the NSPCC Metropolitan Suburb project include parents' activity groups. A two-hour weekly lunchtime group offers a variety of sessions on subjects including art, decorating, child development and health. Parents can take part in more adventurous activities such as canoeing or climbing, while the children have a crèche. The value of the activity group to parents lies partly in meeting others and having a break from the children. However, the educational, fun approach also had results for women who subsequently took up adult education, for which this authority has a strong reputation. Many were studying maths, computing and/or English, and said their confidence had greatly increased as a result. Some were considering further education and/or employment.

'Together Into Play' sessions offered a similar group, activity-based approach for parents to learn about child development, child health, play and learning. A bilingual parents group with a pre-school children's play morning is held where Hindi-, Punjabi-, Urdu- and English-speaking workers are available. Through this group, held in their local health centre, mothers also learnt of and accessed other services such as local authority services for children in school holidays. Ten-week courses are run on subjects such as stress management, how to help with counselling, and handling children's behaviour. Development workers acknowledged that

> while the project set out to work with parents it was mainly mothers who involved themselves. This is an unsurprising reflection of the traditional patterns of childcare...there may be creative ways of involving men and women in opportunities for childcare and training to...enhance the environment.

The project has tried to find these 'creative ways' to involve fathers; a male member of staff has used sports venues to try to get men's groups going. More investment is needed in developing these ideas, and since this research concluded, there has been an internal seminar on developing family support for fathers.

Numbers at the project have grown each year since 1996–1997, when 235 parents and 287 children used it, and many used more than one service. Approximately 52 parents and 65 children used parent activity groups and crèches. Twenty-eight volunteers were trained and 15 parents with 42 children were supported by them, and well over a hundred have now been prepared to help other families.

The Metropolitan Suburb project is based on community development and systems theory. The project workers took the view that dealing with family crisis and stress by one-to-one case work *on its own* is ultimately unworkable, reinforcing a family's isolation and highlighting problem behaviour. Case work can provide a clear framework and child-centred goals, but group and educational approaches can also be used to encourage mutual learning and combat social isolation, as well as to challenge poverty and poor environment, at least in local terms. For example the project arranged the bulk purchasing of some household items. Such an approach has the enormous benefit of encouraging personal and community growth. It does not pretend to cure all underlying structural ills, but it clarifies their nature and potentially gives service users more say in use of resources (see Warren, 1997).

The project's evidence-based approach appears more structured and open to partnership than do earlier models of community work. There is encouraging evidence that the project is meeting at least the short-term support needs, over six months, of mothers and children, in a local authority where levels of children accommodated or on child protection registers are high.

Views of the Project and Its Work

The fact that the NSPCC project was based on the estate it served, and the project manager's energy and courage in speaking out about local issues, had earned respect from local workers:

There are many small local voluntaries and some of the big ones around the area. If an 'outsider organisation' sends in one development worker, they can be lost because there is suspicion about the agenda. But the NSPCC offer services, advice, activities, counselling—that we can refer people to, and they pay rent for our premises.

Community Worker

I think it's an excellent project because it has evolved with the needs of the area. The volunteer visiting helps with isolated parents, encourages them to use services. In adult education we have spent a long time promoting the service, knocking on doors, posting leaflets, and we researched the childcare and adult educational needs of the Black and Asian communities with the (NSPCC) project. That is paying off—we've got a lot of full courses running.

Community Education Officer

Some parents lack understanding of their children's needs. People don't know how to feed a baby or even sterilise a bottle. You give free safety equipment like a fire guard and next week it's gone—sold on. Some parents talk down their children—referring to a four-year-old child as a 'waster', for instance . . . There are plenty of examples of the (NSPCC) volunteers' help, for instance, supporting a mother with agoraphobia to overcome it. Another helped a woman deal with her partner and she is better with the children now.

Health Visitor

Some problems were less tractable:

Women cannot always apply what they have learnt when they get home, especially if the partner is not supportive or is violent. We need services directed at men.

Health Visitor

Thank goodness social services are always there. They tend to be more up front than we are. If people get support at the right time, there need be no more abuse here than any where else. The long-term presence of both statutory and the voluntary services to mediate deprivation is so important.

Health Visitor

Service Users' View of Family Support

Pauline, aged 26, with one child, said:

I do the mum's activity group and the group about playing with children, and I've done three ten-week courses. It has helped me not to get over stressed and to deal with situations—money for instance—better. I wanted somewhere safe for the children, for their well-being; they get good care. Now, rather than shout at (three-year-old) I try to react calmly. For instance, she went down to watch TV one evening and next day the room was like a bomb had hit it. I was ready to fly at her—but instead she went to her room while I cleared up. Plus when my electricity got cut off I was able to come over here.

Stephanie, aged 28, with four children, said:

> *A lot of people associate NSPCC with abuse—but this is a way of showing we are not just about children who are beaten up, but children having a better life, parents getting relief from stress. I have four children and the volunteer help prevents me from being ill. People don't understand how important it is for the little ones to get pre-school education . . . a few parents here care, but many let the children play out late—we had a child of nine over here in her dressing gown asking for a corkscrew late one night. And some children rule the estate.*

Metropolitan Suburb Project: Summary

The NSPCC project's origins lie in community development and action research with local workers and tenants on a large post-war estate. There are pockets of high offending, unemployment and transience, creating the conditions for social exclusion; most parents were concerned for the safety of their children here. The project's research had identified tenants' rejection of being stereotyped as "problem families" and built on their aspirations to access adult education via activity groups and to create a network of trained volunteers. The project budget is £132,000 per annum. The project focusses on parents of pre-school-age children and has made successful efforts to find out about, and respond to, the needs of all sections of the community. It has recently become part of the local Sure Start programme, and its strong community research base will strengthen this development.

METROPOLITAN OUTSKIRTS

Metropolitan Outskirts' project area is on the edge of a large town in the northwest of England, where heavy industry has long been in decline. The area's status is indicated by the presence of a world famous luxury car factory and the fact that hardly anyone on the estate has work there, or indeed work of any kind.

Measuring Economic and Family Stress

The largely rural county is made up of villages, fields and stretches of pre-war council housing on the edge of industrial areas. The county's Research Unit has used national data on income support claimants and compared this with their 'measurements of family stress', which include free school meals, child protection registration, referrals to social services, children looked after, Community Service and Supervision Orders, unemployment and lone parent households. They found the two correlated fairly strongly (Figure 8.3).

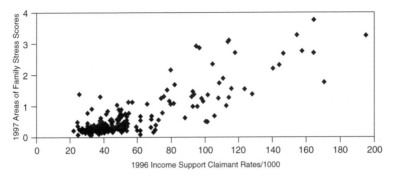

Figure 8.3   1997 areas of family stress compared to 1996 income support claimants

The claimant rate for the county is 27% lower than the national rate, but 6 of its 32 wards have a claimant rate twice as high as the national rate. There are also scattered, densely populated pockets of even higher need, i.e. specific council estates, on one of which the NSPCC project is situated (Figure 8.4). Data on these very local but sharp inequalities are available, but here as elsewhere they are politically sensitive.

Poverty and family stress, measured in a variety of ways, thus appear strongly related and are found in local concentrations, which may be set within or beside areas of relatively far greater affluence. Amenities and shops tend to be located, both geographically and in terms of price, to attract those with spending power. As the value of private housing increases, the families and individuals with least choice become stuck; this includes those made homeless by debt or domestic violence, and those suffering from ill health or depression.

Comments about Metropolitan Outskirts

People whose families were brought up here tend to stay and if you have your family around you can afford to live. There is a lot of prejudice, blaming individuals or groups for the mess, labelling people 'scum', but many people who live here have aspirations for their children.

Refuge Worker

Our neighbour is old, he's very nice. He grows lovely flowers. We use his microwave and he uses our washing machine.

Boy aged 7

The workers build a park for the children but it has been ruined. Some boys pulled off the wooden sign and pushed it over the fence and other children wrote dirty words up.

Girl aged 11

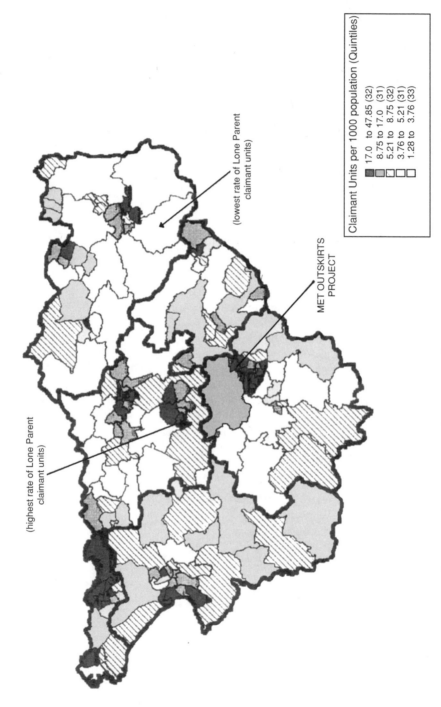

(lowest rate of Lone Parent
claimant units)

MET OUTSKIRTS
PROJECT

(highest rate of Lone Parent
claimant units)

Claimant Units per 1000 population (Quintiles)

17.0 to 47.85 (32)
8.75 to 17.0 (31)
5.21 to 8.75 (32)
3.76 to 5.21 (31)
1.28 to 3.76 (33)

Figure 8.4   Income support lone parents claimant units rates per 1000 population (1996)

The local area could be improved for the children. There is a huge field with a stream needs covering over, and just a climbing frame stuck in the middle hardly used. Kids want hockey, roller blade, and baseball. They could put down a court and parents could provide some of the supervision.

Parent

Where I live is fine. It is safe and I will bring my children up there. Here I feel less safe, it's too rough, children running riot, without enough clothes on, rubbish, glass all over the street. Their parents don't watch out for them. I lived here as a baby and my mum got straight out when someone put a brick through the window. The homes look terrible boarded up.

Parent

A few families can rule an estate and if you don't do as they like, you get out. A travelling family moved in and kept their caravans, then the caravans were torched. One local family runs a second hand metal business in their garden and in the street and no one seems prepared to stop them.

Health Visitor

How the Project was Set Up

The project began in 1994 when members of an NSPCC child protection team about 30 miles away, who knew the area well, decided to do something about the high levels of children in need, and lack of community resources. The team allowed part of their budget and staffing to be used for the development. A terraced council house was provided in 1996, at a peppercorn rent, by the local borough council, and the local NSPCC branch raised £100,000 to run the project for three years. After four years it is now expanding into the adjoining property.

Project Services

The aims of the project are to support families, prevent abuse and to empower the local community. The project offers therapeutic and recovery work from the effects of trauma, as well as support, advice and a safe sanctuary for children and families. What is unusual about this project is that its neighbours can access a number of levels of support just by walking down the street and knocking on the door. For instance, a weekly support group takes place for parents and children. Afterwards some parents buy and prepare lunch jointly. There is a crèche for pre-school children, with explicit service objectives including:

- providing a facility where pre-school children can be left and cared for while parents attend workshops on issues which directly affect their parenting
- providing participating children with a 'high warmth, low criticism' environment in which they can feel free to play and learn

- providing a safe, nurturing and stimulating environment in which each child has an opportunity to advance their physical, intellectual, emotional and speech development in order for them to achieve their full potential.

Similar objectives apply to two after-school clubs run for older children on a weekly basis. The parents' support group acts as a drop-in, so that visitors can have coffee and find out more about the other services being offered without necessarily referring themselves. Parents expressed the view, as in others studies (e.g. Gardner, 1991), that even brief opportunities to leave their own flat or home, to have adult company, to let their child play safely, and to know that support is available if needed, all at minimal cost, are in themselves a perceptible relief of stress.

The support group also provides the opportunity to obtain information about child development and about local services for children and adults, as well as support to access services if they are wanted.

The two staff members, one of whom is a (male) social worker and the other a nursery nurse, also run separate cycles of three-day workshops, for children aged 8–15, for teenage girls aged 14–17 and for women. Each workshop addresses specific issues—'parents under stress'; 'journey to recovery'; 'the inner child.' Each has specific objectives, for instance:

parents under stress: to identify stresses and other factors in parenting; to develop new coping networks that facilitate positive relationships with children and promote listening to children; to help parents develop a positive future for themselves and a high warmth, low criticism environment for their children.

journey to recovery: to provide a group of women survivors of abuse in childhood and/or violence in adulthood with a 'safe place'; to tell their own stories and witness those of others in a non-shaming group; to contribute to their own and others' safe parenting; to reclaim their own potential for recovery from abuse.

inner child: to further develop the 'safe place' established within the previous workshops, using art materials and creativity; to help parents develop positive experiences with their own children by experiencing childhood activities for themselves; to enable parents to make positive choices about their own and their children's futures.

All these workshops are evaluated by exit questionnaires and all are oversubscribed. Some of the men we spoke to who had experienced abuse wanted a similar service. Service users can attend a cycle of workshops more than once, and a few are trained and supported to assist with running them.

From the comments of the parents, children and referring agencies, the perceived success of this model appears to have the following elements:

- Explicit service objectives, including:
  - providing an environment where all communication, including criticism, is as constructive as possible and participants are encouraged to support one another
  - providing opportunity for exploring past or present experiences, whether damaging or otherwise, in a confidential, safe environment, which will allow participants to stop blaming themselves and move on
  - providing access to other opportunities, for example, specialist advice or support, adult education, training as a volunteer, and employment.
- Continuity of staffing, local knowledge and interagency trust.
  Staff had worked in the authority area for some years, and a good level of trust existed between individuals and agencies. For example one of the project staff had worked in the local Social Services. Thresholds for referral were mutually understood.
- Clear professional boundaries and responsibilities in the project.
  These matters were explicit in policy documents, information leaflets, statements of values and conducts, and complaints procedures, which were posted up and readily available.

Because the project was located within the estate, it was seen as extremely important that staff were punctilious about service users' right to confidentiality and privacy, especially that of children. Staff and volunteers did not greet parents they met in the public until they were greeted. The children interviewed knew, and told the researcher, how they could complain to NSPCC's regional office. Children knew, and their parents agreed, that unless their immediate safety was at risk, anything they said would not be quoted outside, including to a member of their own family. They said that this was part of introduction to the project. Staff contacted service users and arranged to see them and explain the centre before a first visit. Staff returned phone calls, notes and messages. There were lapses and mistakes, but service users mentioned these in the context of a service that set and maintained a high standard of communication.

These strict 'rules of conduct', repeatedly stated and followed, might appear overly bureaucratic. The 'rules' gave many parents a sense of respect and safety within the project that was exceptional in their dealings with professionals, and, for a few, also exceptional in their personal lives. The general environment on the estate could be a depressing if not a degrading one, and the project gave a clear message that individuals were valued and should value themselves.

The responsibilities of service users, both adults and children, were also reinforced. Because staff followed the rules, they were able to expect service users to respect one another's confidentiality and not to use abusive language or behaviour. Children who bullied were asked to stop; adults who 'threw a wobbly' were helped to talk it through. If users continued to threaten they could be (and were) temporarily excluded. The highly charged nature of some of the work made these boundaries essential. Responsibilities included an expectation that service users would contribute their skills to the project as far as possible.

One of the NSPCC workers was a community worker with a childcare qualification who had worked in social services and the other was a child protection social worker, and this combination of staff skills allowed for a variety of activities that drew on and extended parents' own competencies and abilities. For instance, organising children's activities or group outings, keeping a financial record for an event, decorating, and writing poetry. Many service users had gone on to assist the project as associates or in running groups as volunteers. Their work is recognised in project literature. Some then used this experience to obtain qualifications and employment.

Social and practical activities could thus be used on their own or combined with the workshops. Some children and adults used the workshops to learn everyday coping skills, such as leaving a room in an argument, rather than hitting. Staff negotiated the work at each stage to ensure that all present were able to participate fully and not feel threatened. Disclosures about bullying, domestic violence or years of sexual abuse were also made. Staff members were trained to listen to these disclosures and to help the group to support one another. Play, storytelling, role-play and creative work such as art and writing are all used to help participants express themselves—often after years of suppressing past abuse because of shame and low self-esteem. They took responsibility and action as necessary, successfully supporting the victim through court appearance in some cases. Although the majority of those attending were women, many boys also used the groups and several non-abusing men had referred or helped their partners to attend. The fact that one of the workers was male made this much easier, as he was able to model supportive, safe male behaviour.

The broad spectrum of services accessible through one site meant that families did not have to be or remain a 'problem' in order to get help. Individuals could *move back and forth* from difficult and cathartic exploration of past victimisation, where they suffered psychologically and needed much skilled support, to developing new skills of their own. For many this was the first good learning experience they could remember; ultimately they could apply knowledge and qualities acquired, to help others and/or to move on to new and creative fields of work and leisure.

Views of the Project

Both project workers said that the NSPCC 'brand name' had been a mixed blessing. Some local people had been suspicious about parents being 'watched'. However, NSPCC had given them status and professionalism in the best sense. Above all they felt they had been trusted by NSPCC to develop the project:

> *we have done it our own way—not just crisis intervention, but all kinds of activities to empower children and parents so they see they can change things themselves.*
> NSPCC project worker

In the view of other local professionals, the fact that one project worker had been known in the area for years, and both had the respect of local agencies, made an enormous difference

> *they have done so much here and are so well respected.*
> Community Worker

> *It is excellent that the team is a man and a woman and that they work so well together.*
> Health Visitor

> *I have known (project workers) all my working life and we keep in touch about any worries.*
> Social Worker

This degree of continuity of experience and trust, both within the NSPCC and between local workers, meant that the Metropolitan Outskirts project had been able to structure the service to fit gaps in other provision. They knew where to refer people to get specialist help with the minimum delay.

Service Users' Views of the Project

What follows is a selection of quotations from parents, to illustrate their use of family support to work through their own difficulties and damaging experiences and to resolve some of the problems their children were facing. The difficulties included experience of abuse, lack of consistent parenting as a child, violence in a relationship, acute or chronic health problems including mental health, or a combination of all these. Children's problems included being abused, social isolation, extreme hyperactivity treated with drugs, destructive or violent behaviour, being bullied, eating problems, and anxiety.

Parents were concerned to get social and emotional support for children directly, either to prevent problems arising or to prevent deterioration. They felt they had not received much support from adolescent mental health services

ces, who were hard to access, although social workers made
.s to the project. Schools 'held on' to children's behaviour but
similar difficulties obtaining specialist support prior to exclusion

.   valued having a range of services available, which included informal social drop-in; advice for their children and/or as a parent; and
specialised, intensive help available without lengthy referral, to deal with past
or present trauma. Most parents accepted that serious concerns about their
own parenting might be reported by the NSPCC to social services and/or
the police. Those who had this experience said that they had been supported
by the NSPCC in improving their parenting and continued to receive family support from the NSPCC throughout the child protection process. What
is impressive about the following anonymised quotations is the amount of
learning they demonstrate. We need to establish whether and, if so, how, such
learning is consolidated and used by parents over the long term.

Abuse and Domestic Violence

Diana, aged 36, with two children, described repeated experiences of serious
assault:

> We were strapped as children, the children were stood in a corner and told not to answer
> back; I remember my brother black and blue from it. I moved around with my husband's
> work for many years and he got violent. I left him with the children after 18 years
> and went into a refuge. I have had a detached retina and now I'm told I have multiple
> sclerosis. I am pregnant by the man I moved in with.

She related her daughter's anxiety to having witnessed domestic violence:

> Ann is eleven, she is very protective—she shoots out into the road to stop her younger
> sister who is deaf, but then sticks the baby under her arm like a doll—I have to tell her
> it's not safe. She pretends to have tummy ache at school time and gets in a terrible state,
> after I say she can stay home she is fine again.

She saw the NSPCC project as providing help both for herself and Ann:

> this is a place for the children. Whatever happens to them as children, they have for
> the rest of their lives, so it is better to them to shrug it off now. Coming here helps me
> handle them better. Here they have more freedom, if they get paint on the walls it is not
> a disaster. So it is a release for me as well.

Diana thought the project had provided her with alternatives to displaying
anger, and she had broken the pattern of physical abuse:

People say to me 'you're a good mum, you know all about it'—but no one knows what happens when the door is shut, do they? Many times I felt like hitting her, but I didn't, I thought 'If I do that I'm no better than him.' He hit me, not them, he was good with children generally, he just shouted at them. Now, I stop the children's treats rather than shout at them.

Mary, aged 38, is in a second marriage with three children from her first marriage. She also described a history of abuse:

I was abused as a child and in a violent first marriage. It scared the life out of me when my (second) husband made the referral. He went to the Citizen's Advice and they told him about this project. He was scared he might hit my 18-year-old daughter. My 12-year-old has a lovely side to him but he can go on a 'hyper' in the morning and he won't go to school.

She found that the NSPCC addressed her need to deal with her experiences, as well as her children's needs:

I needed to come to terms with what had happened to me and the NSPCC workshops helped me to do it. I was not at ease with myself. I lacked confidence. I would not go to social services because I used to be in care, and my first husband used to threaten the kids with going into care. I now volunteer here and my daughter helps with the after school club; she's good with people. I think she will go a long way. My son goes to the after school club, so long as he's taken there, and his confidence is picking up now.

Mary's second husband, John, was interviewed separately and told of the crisis that made him seek help:

I wanted to get help for my wife, but the breaking point came when her 18-year-old kept on winding me up and telling me to hit her. I grabbed her and pushed her against the wall and pulled back my arm. It was a very dangerous position. Then I punched the wall instead and broke my knuckles. I spent six weeks in a sling. My stepdaughter admitted she wanted her dad back with her mum. So I went to the Citizen's Advice Bureau and explained and they sent me down here.

His view was that there would have been more violence unless he and his wife had received help quickly:

the eldest has eating problems and goes back and forth to her father—the other two are doing well, the boy has just blossomed. I know other people think NSPCC has a stigma—that 'they will take your child away'—but they are there to help—I've only found this out got here. After the incident, I was a bit frightened, I thought 'I need someone to know—I've got to explain this'. Instead of being a nervous wreck my wife is brimming with confidence now. She is going to start a job. So we are beginning to get there as a family.

Eileen, aged 26, has two children. She described her history. She too needed to deal with the effects of earlier abuse, and take action to bring the perpetrator to justice.

> *I was abused from age six to 16. Recently, I got very depressed and when I came here I told them about it. We went to court and he was found guilty. I knew my partner would not be able to cope and, once he knew, he left me. Only the children stopped me killing myself. My seven-year-old is very loud at times. He has definite difficulties—is restless, has tantrums, is often worried—it's quite stressful for me. My partner now is very supportive. I met (the NSPCC worker) at a playgroup where she gave out information and I heard about the therapeutic workshops. It needs more places like this. Some people have been to the groups run by Social Services. It is not necessarily a bad experience there but this is more homely. You are careful about confidentiality, to leave things at the door when you go out. So you don't just walk up to a mother you've seen here, if she is with a friend somewhere else.*

Eileen felt the project had relieved stress and allowed her and the children to start enjoying life more:

> *I want my life back; to be happy, and for the children to be happy. They go to the NSPCC after-school club. At first some people thought NSPCC had moved here to take children away—it felt like a stigma. But the people who work here have dealt with adults and children in awkward situations and—they understand—problems with kids and partners. My mother said 'why are you going there? They will keep an eye on your kids'. It's not like that—it is to keep the family together. I wish it had been here when I was little. I have become a volunteer and worked with the crèche and workshops here; I'm qualified with the local council to work with children. I am not so depressed—I go line dancing once a week.*

Serious Behaviour Problems

Molly, a grandmother aged 56, described what she saw as the consequences of a family history of abuse, and an immediate experience of violence and insecurity, for her grandchildren:

> *my grandchild Jane is nine years old and was in a Refuge for three months when she was five, and for three months last year. Her mother has had three violent partners and Jane is violent to her sister and brothers, and when she is restrained she kicked the wardrobes in at the refuge. Even so, she is top of the class in reading. Her brother is seven—he has Oppositional Defiance Disorder, it's like ADHD but Ritalin doesn't work. He watched his mother being raped. He is in a special unit now—calming down a bit. These problems have been passed on I believe, I was abused as a child and I was so ashamed of myself, I married the first man who came along and he did the same to my daughters. Only one of my daughters did the same though. I think it can be stopped for my grandchildren, now they are getting help. It shocked me when my grandson came to the workshop and said 'what makes me sad? Seeing my dad strangling my mum'.*

In order to support her daughter's family she herself needed support:

volunteering makes me feel better and I am putting something back for all the help NSPCC gave me. For me it is 'maintenance' support—keeping me on an even keel when I get low. For Jane—she can get her emotions expressed, her bad experiences, and it leaves room for her to have a normal life and be a little girl, to achieve more. It's the only place I know where children can get this out and it is not judged too horrible to hear—the only place you get affirmed as a good parent. It is about changing perceptions, recognising that people need help in a safe place without thinking your child might be snatched. Prevention sums it up. To us it felt as though Social Services was more interested in evidence for a conviction than in support or keeping us informed. I go and help with their training for child protection workers now.

Summary: Metropolitan Outskirts Project

This is a community-based project in a terraced house on a council estate, in a local area of high family need. It offers open facilities such as a drop-in, a crèche and an after-school club. There are outings and activities for families so that fathers and children not directly involved can join in. The budget is £100,000 over three years.

More intensive groups and workshops for children and adults are also available, dealing with confidence building, parenting problems and skills, and experiences such as childhood abuse or domestic violence. There are only two full-time staff members but their combined skills and local knowledge, as well as the use of trained volunteers, means parents can access a wide spectrum of services on the spot.

Because of the sensitive nature of the work and its location in the community, the rules of conduct for staff and service users are very clear and appear to be respected.

Parents' and professionals' comments indicate that they value the project because family members can move from general to specialised support and back, without lengthy and anxiety-provoking procedures. Children's comments indicate that they gain confidence and enjoy the activities, particularly non-stressful attention from adults.

NEW ESTATE

The project is located in a family centre on an island of public housing. It is a London overspill estate built by the Greater London council in the 1960s. Surrounding it is mixed, mostly privately owned, housing on the edge of a shire county town. The contrast between the estate and the local area is similar to that in Metropolitan Outskirts, but the public housing here is newer and has been refurbished by a Housing Association since the mid 1990s. The NSPCC project is again in an area of relatively greater deprivation.

Unemployment in the local ward was near to the national average in 1999 at 4.5%, whereas the county average was much lower, at just 2.8%. The ward also scores higher than most others in the northern half of this large county on the Jarman index, which measures social deprivation.

In a county with high educational attainment overall, where 14.5% of over 18 years are qualified, just 4% are qualified in this ward. Over a third of pupils in the local primary school are eligible for free school meals and nearly half (45.1%) have been identified as having special educational needs—well over the national average.

The economic recession of the early 1990s, when jobs disappeared while interest rates rose, had a serious impact in this area. Many families moved on to the estate following repossession of their homes. Families split up under the pressure and effectively became homeless. The term 'doing your time on the estate' is used, because the housing association requires tenants to stay for two years before they can apply for a transfer. Nevertheless, efforts have been made to improve the quality of life. The use of entrance phones and surveillance has reduced crime, while the community association and NSPCC Family Centre have encouraged some people out of their isolation. Many tenants still feel resentment that they have lost, or cannot afford, their own home in a relatively affluent area, and do not want to identify with the life of the estate.

Comments about New Estate

I've lived here for eleven years and like it. I know all the places to take children and which are least expensive. There's a recreation centre and ballpark, hockey rink, roller-skating. It would help if people shared the use of cars more then you could get to the seaside for instance. There needs to be more for the teenagers—there isn't even a cinem here.

Parent

Ever since people were moved here by the GLC it's had a social stigma and it's the first stop after bed and breakfast even now. If you went for a job from this estate, even with the same qualifications, you would not get it if they knew your address.

Parent

The Residents' Association has started up again, they got 20 people to a public meeting—not bad at all—and organised a Youth Café and discos for the kids in the holiday. People are willing to try to make a difference for themselves and for the community.

NSPCC Worker

Five years ago we had to go out in pairs on visits. There was active drug trafficking and the stairwells were soiled and dangerous. Vandalism cost so much they put in cameras, security doors and a 24-hour concierge. It has worked—but it will take longer for the estate's reputation to match the reality.

Social Worker

It's a bit of a jungle out there. Parents who own their houses don't want their children at primary school with children from the estate. Middle class parents tend to move their children on to a different junior school at seven.

Head Teacher

Whether it's a good place to live, depends on who you are. Money and employment make the difference to family stability.

Parent

How the Project was Set Up

The family centre originated from a child protection unit set up by the NSPCC in 1984. At that time, all NSPCC child protection officers were qualified social workers and, unusually in a largely female profession, they were predominantly men. The local 'cruelty man', as he was known, was remembered more affectionately than this nickname would suggest. He knocked on doors looking for bruises, but also worked with community groups, built a team of family support workers and helped local families in need. The wives of NSPCC child protection officers were also some of the first (unpaid) community and family support workers—literally the 'other half' of NSPCC's work with children at risk and in need.

Purpose-built premises were offered to the NSPCC at a low rent by the local housing association, in the mid-1990s. These include offices, kitchen, interview rooms and a large playroom and hall. There are seven staff, all but two being part-time and equivalent to four full-time staff. They have qualifications in social work, counselling and nursery nursing. Local agencies provide staff time to help run specific services. Health visitors, an early years worker, an educational psychologist and local authority workers from a family centre offer sessions. The overall budget is £140,000 per annum, a relatively low cost for a family centre.

Project Services

The current manager decided to focus the service on children under eight and their parents. Family support is offered through a series of more or less structured parent-training courses, with parallel provision for children.

The benefits of these structured sessions are that:

- they have clear overall aims and specific objectives for each session, so that parents know what to expect of the staff—and of themselves—and can make a better informed choice about whether they want the service
- evaluation is clearer and as a result, modifying and improving the programme is easier

- the content relates to specific instances of child and/or carer behaviour, and therefore, according to carers, is often easier to manage than general advice when they are under stress. They are clear about trying to achieve change in one area of difficulty; success in that area increases confidence to widen the horizon for change to other aspects of family relationships.

The project's work programme is strongly research-based, drawing on the work of Eyberg and Matarazzo (1980), Forehand *et al.* (1984) and Webster-Stratton and Herbert (1994). The manager undertook a doctoral thesis on the effectiveness of parent-training groups and this research, comparing two different types of parent support with a control group who received neither, suggested that 'the method seemed less important than parents' understanding, commitment and mutual support' (Gill, 1998). In 1995, the family centre started to use the Parent–Child Game, developed in the United States and used in the United Kingdom at the Maudsley Hospital's Family Assessment Unit. Its aim is to work collaboratively with parents in helping them to understand what might be reinforcing child behavioural problems, especially non-compliance or defiance, and how, in a child-centred way, they can encourage alternative positive behaviour. The approach includes:

- observation and rating of parent–child interaction
- microphone and ear-bug link to parent
- modelling and role-play
- play work
- review and feedback
- weekly tasks to ensure skills are transferred to the home.

The aim is to improve parental skills with children and to reduce child behavioural problems, hopefully also reducing stress levels in the family. Staff and volunteers, including parents, have the opportunity to undertake training and to participate in running the programme. This brings a range of skills and experience to the service and also offers self-development opportunities to those involved. It shows parents that they are not passive 'recipients' but can also become providers, an important contribution to building trust and self-esteem, as well as to the family centre's resources.

The service consists of an initial assessment followed by five sessions of structured work on *attending* to a child (when a parent notices what a child does without questioning or criticising), *rewarding, ignoring, giving directions* and *time out*. There is a manual for those presenting the sessions, which last for 1 hour a week with two workers; they can be provided in or out of the home setting and the game can be adapted to individual children's needs.

During the research, we found family support services to be increasingly research-based, prepared and delivered by partner agencies, and evaluated.

New Estate has evaluated parental attitudes to discipline, to parenting and the child/ren, and the child's behaviour, using the Eyberg Child Behaviour Inventory (Eyberg and Matarazzo, 1980), and parents' views before and after intervention. While *attitudes* to discipline had not altered significantly, *methods* of dealing with different behaviour *and the behaviour itself* had changed in the carers' view, in over half the cases, and this change was maintained after three months. The providers add that 'overall, the mental health of these families has improved, with positive effect for all members. It is hypothesised that improved parenting skills will prevent future child behaviour problems and act as a buffer to external stress'. Our study further reinforces this hypothesis.

NSPCC staff routinely evaluated their services for user satisfaction. On New Estate and elsewhere those who had a research interest or experience were more adventurous with evaluation methods, particularly with children. They collaborated with other professions such as educational psychology, more often. In other words, they appeared to feel freer and less risk–averse, when it came to learning from practice.

New Estate project also ran an eight-week group course for parents to obtain mutual support and learn techniques in handling everyday problems with children, such as temper tantrums and attention–seeking, without using physical punishment. The 'Confident Parents, Confident Kids' course is run with the educational psychology service. It covers:

- understanding your child's needs
- being a parent
- causes of difficult behaviour
- playing with your child
- setting boundaries
- teaching your child good behaviour.

Again the staff used the Eyberg inventory to evaluate effectiveness. Parents reported an average of over three difficult behaviours per child before the course, reducing to one afterwards. In all the services, the maintenance over time of reported benefits would require follow-up for a longer time.

The 'Happy Families Group' is a similar service for parents of infants, run with the health-visiting service. Staff evaluation indicated some positive results from parents' reports, both for themselves in terms of confidence and in terms of a reduction in difficulties presented by the child. The 'Hand Prints' School Learning Programme is a year's intensive programme structuring the activities of the centre crèche. It aims to prepare pre-school children to 'flourish at school', much in the spirit of the Sure Start programme, by teaching small children skills such as learning together through play, co-operating, listening, holding a pencil and sitting still. We found that parents whose primary aim in seeking day care was preparing children for school, were enthusiastic. They were transferring some of the taught skills to school-age children, so that the service is now being extended to 5–8-year-olds at the 'Dinosaur School', focusing on their social skills.

The project is demonstrably addressing family support at a number of levels:

- improving children's own skills in handling their environment and expressing their needs
- improving the parent–child relationship
- building parental confidence and skills in negotiating with the child rather than simply using pressure
- enabling parents to deal with adult relationship difficulties using family group work and advocacy for those negotiating with other agencies or who have a disability that makes communication difficult.

Finally, at the community level, the family centre offers a venue and access to the community centre, an annual play scheme for 250 children and seasonal events.

A consultation exercise on new services, the results of which are reported back to parents, and a breakdown of referrals showing the broad nature of the work indicate that this centre is fulfilling its mission statement 'working with the local community to offer help and support to families'.

Views of the Project

Professionals described the kinds of difficulties faced by families on the estate: relative poverty, isolation from family and friends, depression, and emotional harm to, or neglect of, children.

> It can be very harsh for some children—you see them out playing alone from age two, or caring for a younger sibling when they are still very young.
>
> Health Visitor

> Some of the parents are not well parented themselves. They give material things but do not cuddle or talk. They ask the teacher 'when will you teach him to respect me?'
>
> Head Teacher

Local agencies saw some of the symptoms:

> We get very high scores on the Edinburgh Post Natal Depression Scale, particularly lone mothers who have been homeless.
>
> Health Visitor

> The baseline assessment shows our children tend to be poor on language and social skills. They can get to Level Two but they struggle with Level Three, to write imaginatively.

The boys are now doing as well as girls and we think it is because we provide a clear structure—we don't accept refusal to do the work.

Head Teacher

There is a high referral of child protection work from this area—it is all high priority so we have done no preventative work ourselves for over a year.

Social Worker

Asked for evidence of the projects effectiveness, professionals gave a number of specific examples of change, which they attributed to its work:

NSPCC has built up the mother's confidence and the home has been safer for the child—so we have been able to take children's names off the child protection register.

Social Worker

I see mothers more confident and 'back in charge' instead of defeated—they acquire new skills after 6–8 weeks here. I would not send them if I did not see it work.

Health Visitor

I see the child's behaviour improve because the parent has been helped to cope with the difficulty he presents.

Head Teacher

Views about the national image of the NSPCC were more mixed. Some NSPCC staff shared these concerns:

the abuse publicity can create barriers for some families who have real problems.

Health Visitor

I think NSPCC should do more to publicise its success in preventing harm in families' hard work. The current publicity puts off some people who could use their help.

Teacher

NSPCC is seen differently to Social Services, who are required to see the family. NSPCC has an informal basis which remains strong enough to allow it to maintain a good relationship while they do child protection work, and we often co-work together.

Social Worker

Service Users' Views

I am a lone father bringing up my daughter. I want to understand her needs and get my worries answered—they are good at that. When she is five I won't be eligible for a service anymore, that worries me but I will pop in for advice if I need it. I am going on the Parenting course and my three-year-old will be at a crèche. She is making friends coming to meet other children, and I have made one or two as well.

After six months, he said:

I think I am able to trust people more and they trust me—also my little girl is getting ready for school, and so am I, for her going there.

A mother with three children said:

> *I'm on my own with the children—I wanted the toddler to have friends, not be cooped up with me, and I wanted advice on how to handle the other's temper tantrums—at four she could wreck her room. I had a stormy marriage and then a breakdown after my daughter was born. So I'm doing the Confident Parents, Confident Children course, and my daughter comes to a structured playgroup.*

And after six months:

> *It has made a difference to my approach to the children. They definitely help you to avoid using desperate measures. I have re-thought discipline, instead of shouting now, I praise the other one and he stops playing up. Also my daughter does not wreck the room any more. Her concentration and communication are improving. The school were worried about my seven-year-old boy's behaviour—its sexual content—so he has had some counselling here. They may interview him in case he has been abused. He is bedwetting and running out of school. But the sexual behaviour is not so bad now. I can trust them over child protection and although Social Services have been involved they came here to the NSPCC project so I felt more secure.*

Summary: New Estate Project

This is a Family Centre, in purpose-built accommodation on a 1960s estate. It has one full-time manager and three part-time workers; the budget is approximately £140,000 per annum. In a relatively affluent area, many households suffered loss of employment and private housing in the recession of the 1980–1982 and some split up.

The centre works predominately with parents of pre-school children. It provides a crèche for infants and more structured play for pre-school children. This is so popular that it is being extended to school-age children, developing their social skills.

Parents receive structured, evaluated courses giving techniques for dealing with specific developmental stages and difficulties. Practitioner evaluations indicated that parents' and children's behaviour had been modified even if parents' attitudes to discipline had not changed—in other words, those that used physical punishment had not needed to do so to the same degree. Again, parents were transferring skills learnt for use with young children to their older siblings.

Like the other projects, this one also maintains a range of services, offering open community use of the centre for meetings and holiday play sessions at one end of the spectrum. The bulk of families use the play facilities for children and the parenting skills groups. Where there were specific family problems some one-to-one counselling was offered and support in dealing with other agencies, for example support in a child protection investigation.

Unfortunately, this project was closed in the reorganisation of NSPCC services. It is hoped this research will enable its work to benefit other family support initiatives.

This chapter has given examples of family support practice of a kind generally pioneered in the voluntary sector and now incorporated into national programmes. With regard to the content of services, these include:

- adult education and personal development for parents
- parenting skills training
- play therapy and play skills
- open access services, e.g. drop-in, outings, information days, sometimes alongside
- specialist services, e.g. domestic violence, grief counselling
- advocacy and negotiation skills, e.g. dealing with professionals
- parent involvement in provision, e.g. volunteering
- working with fathers and the extended family
- community outreach and development.

With regard to the structure and rationale of the service, examples include:

- multi-skilled teams
- mixed funding sources
- developing policy and practice on child safety in the community
- links to multi-agency forums on family support and child protection
- increasing diversity of, and access to, services in the community
- incorporating evaluation into practice development.

9

CHILDREN IN NEED AND LOCAL SERVICES

This chapter gives a wider context to six NSPCC projects' work with families. It provides information on children in need and children in need of protection (see below for legal definitions of these groups), for the six local authorities in question, and on the services being provided for them. This information has been drawn from a number of sources. A part of this has been taken from Children's Plans, documents drawn up by the local authority with its partner health authority (or authorities, where more than one is involved), with contributions from many service providers including voluntary organisations. Such plans have been mandatory since 1996.

Section 31 of the Children Act 1989 deals with "harm" as follows:

"harm" means ill-treatment or the impairment of health or development;
"development" means physical, intellectual, emotional, social or be-
haviytural development;
"health" means physical or mental health; and
"ill-treatment" includes sexual abuse and forms of ill-treatment which are
not physical.

The Children Act 1989 section 17 defines a child as being "in need" if:

(a) he is unlikely to achieve or maintain, or have the opportunity of achieving or maintaining, a reasonable standard of health or development without the provision for him of services by the local authority;
(b) his health or development is likely to be significantly impaired, or further impaired, without the provision of such services; or
(c) he is disabled.

Central Government now requires local authorities in England to produce extensive data for its Quality Protects initiative. Children's services have set

Table 9.1   MAP data for the six study authorities (2000–2001)

Local Authority for	Met S	Met O	New Est	Sea S	Inner C	Garden C
CH under 18	73,625	233,230	298,847	175,000	36,736	162,902
CIN inc. CLA	7973	X	7150	3600	3177	2700
% Non-White	11	1	X	5.36	42	11.3
CPR	399	322	364	537	145	250
% Non-White	X	13.6	X	4.5	21	5.1
CLA	448	674	660	820	340 (41 UAS)	537
CIN/CLA	X	X	X	X	X	X
% Non-White	X	X	X	6.1	46	12.9
Adoption plan	50	X	61	35	40	50
% Non-White	X	X	X	9.1	54	8
Categories of *CIN*						
1. Abuse/neglect	X	X	X	1582	431	670
2. Disability	2284	2300	8447	590	346	630
3. Parental Illness/ disability	X	X	X	149	120	120
4. Acute stress	X	X	X	291	517	260
5. Family dysfunction	X	X	X	607	613	180
6. Socially unacceptable behaviour	X	X	X	268	124	250
7. Low income	X	X	X	45	849	160
8. Absent parenting	X	X	X	58	177	430

Notes:
X, information unavailable; UAS, unaccompanied asylum seekers; CIN, children in need (Children Act 1989, s 17); CLA, children looked after (Children Act 1989, s 20); CPR, child protection register.

out baseline data from 1998 and targets for subsequent years to 2002, as well as management actions achieved and planned to attain national and local targets. There is further discussion of this process in Chapter 10. We have drawn on these Management Action Plans (MAPs), which are public documents. Local authorities provide other annual data returns to the Department of Health and some of this information has been used. For comparative purposes, we show a selection of data on children in need and child protection across all six authorities, in Tables 9.1 and 9.2. Gaps indicate a lack of available data at the time of writing.

In relation to children in need of protection, we bring in information from annual reports provided by each local authority's Area Child Protection Committee (ACPC). The ACPC is a strategic group made up of representatives of local agencies working with children. Its role is to oversee child protection services and ensure that they are well coordinated and effective.

The demography of the six local authority areas is very different in some respects, but the immediate project localities are much more similar to one

Table 9.2 Child protection registration—data for the six study authorities

Year ending 31/3/99	London	England	Met S	Met O	New E	Sea S	Inner C	Garden C
Children registered/deregistered numbers	3805/3832	30,100/29,600	322/395	258/225	499/480	498/377	117/114	272/261
Children registered/deregistered rate per 10,000 population	23/23	27/26	43/53	17/15	18/17	30/23	39/38	18/18
Category neglect number	1682	10,100	85	62	160	185	58	73
Category neglect rate per 10,000 population	10	9	11	4	6	11	19	5
Category physical injury number	737	7000	71	15	141	177	22	69
Category physical injury rate per 10,000 population	4	6	9	1	5	5	7	5
Category sexual abuse number	407	4300	78	2	60	93	4	51
Category sexual abuse rate per 10,000 population	1	4	10	0	2	3	1	7
Category emotional abuse number	4800	578	88	33	76	127	28	39
Emotional abuse rate per 10,000	4	4	12	2	3	8	9	3
Ranked rate of registration (1 = highest)			1	5	4	3	2	4
Ranked rate of deregistration (1 = highest)			1	6	5	3	2	4

another, representing relatively greater (if not always the greatest) levels of need and disadvantage for their area. To provide local colour, and independent data, we have also used illustrative material from Joint Reviews by the Social Services Inspectorate and the Audit Commission, where these were available. The reviews, published regularly by the Stationery Office, evaluate records, statistics and interviews and provide an independent assessment of how well the public is being served by services locally. We hope the result of using a variety of sources is a picture that, while still incomplete, indicates the complexity and diversity of policy and practice issues that lie behind the rather dry figures.

CHILDREN IN NEED IN GARDEN CITY

In the Garden City Authority, out of approximately 163,000 children and young people aged under 18, a conservative estimate of children in need is approximately 1.7% or 2700, including approximately 300 children registered as in need of a protection plan. A further 200–300 children, presumably cases where child protection enquiries are being made, are the subject of 'active concern about abuse and neglect', and 260 are 'families under acute stress'.

Service Developments for Children in Need

The county's MAP 2000–2001 gives a self-assessment of strengths and weaknesses in each topic covered by the Plan. With regard to children in need, strengths are seen as a 'culture of collaboration' and 'community-based initiatives'. Three such initiatives are illustrated as examples of good practice with children in need in Garden City, albeit on a relatively small scale. Of these, one is an initiative to support care-leavers, a second is a self-help group for women who have suffered domestic violence, and the third is a service for families with an autistic child supported by one full-time equivalent worker. As elsewhere (see p. 135 and p. 139), a multi-disciplinary team has been set up to offer a response to adolescents with severe behavioural problems. This response is due to be extended to a younger age group, but the process for evaluation is not outlined. The Action Plan's assessment of weaknesses includes 'lack of commissioning capacity for development of services for children in need' and 'underdevelopment of work with children from black and ethnic minorities', although there is potential for such work from within primary care teams in the health service.

The county for Garden City had also, since its last plan, developed an authority-wide project to 're-focus' services towards family support and held an inter-agency family support conference to develop locality action plans.

The Audit Commission/Social Services Inspectorate Joint Review considered that to be effective, funding and ownership of this development needed to be improved, and that 'in such a high profile area, it is imperative that management responsibilities and accountability are clear and unequivocal'.

Rather like Metropolitan Outskirts' 'Family Strength Index,' the county has developed a 'young persons support index' to assist in measuring need, using indicators associated with the risk of children being taken into care (Bebbington and Miles, 1989). The ward for the project and its neighbouring ward are among the 10 showing the greatest levels of need in the county on these indicators. These include:

- single-parent family
- over four children in family
- ethnic group
- tenure, private rented
- tenure, council rated
- overcrowding
- child's age
- benefits.

The county carried out a study in mid-2000 to map needs by identifying families known to social services, where a wide range of factors were present, including:

- economic difficulties and debt
- domestic violence
- substance misuse
- physical disability
- learning difficulty
- mental health
- lone parents
- young parents
- children who are truant
- children excluded from school
- children from large families.

Social workers in Referral and Assessment and Family Support teams were asked to identify relevant factors in each open case. Across the county, the average number of family stress factors per open case was 4.4, but the highest number was 5.2, in the Garden City area of the county. Concerns about abuse and neglect were highest in this area. There were also high relative levels of concern about lone parents and parents with mental health problems, as well as about possibly dangerous adults living with children and offending

Table 9.3   Percentages for the Garden City on each factor and the county average

	Garden City	County (average)
Debt	33	29
Housing problems	40	29
Domestic violence	37	31
Alcohol abuse	22	19
Drug abuse	19	15
Learning difficulties (parent)	14	11
Learning difficulties (child)	13	10
Mental health (parent)	28	19
Mental health (child)	12	9
Lone parent	52	41
Offending behaviour (parent)	23	19
Risky adults	13	10
Persistent truants	14	10
Concern reabuse/neglect	63	58
Average number of factors in each case	5.2	4.4

behaviour by parents. The percentages for the project area, Garden City, on each factor and the county average are given in Table 9.3. Although somewhat different measures are used in different authorities, greater levels of family need are seen in the project neighbourhoods of all the projects we researched, compared with the authorities' populations of children in need, reinforcing the data presented in Chapter 8. It has to be remembered that children in need are themselves just under 2% of children in this authority, and so the high-scoring cases are likely to contain children at high risk of developmental impairment.

This comparative study gives a helpful insight into the work of the statutory agencies and the population of families in need in the local authority for Garden City. Open cases are mapped by postcode and are clustered tightly in neighbourhoods, one of which is that of the NSPCC project. The data could be a powerful tool for targeting specific types of local family support. Work can now be undertaken to gather evidence on successful interventions for specific groups where there is believed to be high need, for instance, families where carers have serious mental health problems, disability, learning difficulties or problems with substance abuse.

In relation to the area of the NSPCC project, The MAP states that, worryingly, there is 'potential for a number of developments, but no tangible progress, due to lack of leadership, lack of inter-agency cooperation and lack of resources'. This is despite an increase by 3% in expenditure on children in need, not including those looked after. It is of interest that an 'underdevelopment of family support services and the inadequate assessment of emotional abuse and neglect' are identified as weaknesses of the child protection system for the county. Unfortunately, the special grant for work under the Quality Protects initiative (over £1 million in this county) has many fewer targets applying to children in need in the community than for children who are already in need of protection or are away from home.

Children in Need of Protection

There were 250 children on the Child Protection Register in the Garden City authority as of March 1999 (MAP). By September of that year, the number had risen to 412 (ACPC Report). If these figures are accurate, they pose a potential problem for the county to reduce the number to 250 children by 2002 as intended, and if inaccurate, they reveal inconsistency in data collection. Although deregistration of children who have been on the child protection register for over two years is speeding up, other indicators such as re-registrations and reviews are 'in the wrong direction'. This signals a pressure building up in the system. Performance management and more targeted activity alone may not contain underlying problems such as increased demand in response to child protection concerns, staff vacancies or sickness.

Area Child Protection Committee (ACPC) data indicates that the county town (of which the project area forms a part) has 129 children on the register, which constituted over 40% of the registrations in the county as of September 2000. Data on each aspect of child protection registration in this local authority is gathered for different geographical divisions, frustrating comparison across the authority. Sexual abuse accounted for nearly one fifth of all single-category registrations (19.7%) in September 1999. Registrations using more than one category of harm, discouraged by the Department of Health, accounted for over a third (33%). If these are broken down, we see that emotional harm at 29% and physical harm at 25% made up the largest proportion of multiple-category registrations, with sexual abuse still high at 23%.

Children in Ethnic and Other Minority Groups

As in other local authorities, the MAP (2000–2001) for Garden City gives the figure of children receiving a service at a given point—2700—as the figure for children in need, including children looked after and supported independently. The Plan does not break down the total number but gives the percentage of children belonging to ethnic groups 'other than White' (the figure requested) as 11.3%; the ethnic minority population of the county (1991 figures) was 7.4%.

The MAP also gives the percentage of looked-after children from ethnic 'non-White' backgrounds as 12.9%, reducing to 8% for prospective adoptions, and a similar proportion (8%) of children with disabilities. These figures indicate that tertiary prevention with children from ethnic minorities, returning them to the community from local authority accommodation, appears to be relatively successful, but we would have to look at the ages of the children and whether they in fact go on to other institutions. Children from specific (including mixed heritage) ethnic backgrounds make up 4.2% of children on the child protection register, with 'other' or 'unknown' 11.6%.

The figures need to be broken down into ethnic groups and localities, since the census shows most Black Caribbean and Indian families living in two or three of the county's 148 wards. Between 11% and 15.8% is a substantial group or groups, yet there is little in the MAP about improving services for children of ethnic minorities. Targets for children with a disability include mention of 'a joint project with a local Black community organisation to look at needs, and the way the Directorate responds'.

The local authority plans to improve data on families in need, by gathering more information on those currently in receipt of services and developing a clearer profile in order to target resources. It also seeks locality information, and has weighted wards across the county in relation to potential need, from the least needy at −2895 points, to the most at plus +11,471 points, the theoretical average being 200. Again, wide inequalities are apparent. The highest weighting is in the area adjacent to the NSPCC project where 'a post funded from the Quality Protects grant is developing inter-agency family support initiatives and conducting more detailed analysis of need':

Specific groups about which there are concerns include:

- children of mixed parentage apparently over-represented on the Child Protection Register and in the looked-after population;
- children with a degree of autism;
- children with a diagnosis of Attention Deficit with Hyperactivity; and
- teenage parents.

Our research touched on many of these concerns. There appears to be high quality data on need in this county, but it is poorly coordinated and inaccessible to the managers who could use it.

Summary: The Local Authority's Response to Children in Need in Garden City

It was difficult to obtain information on this authority's services, although this appeared to be a problem of organisation and public relations rather than lack of transparency. Once data was made available, it appeared there had been some interesting work on mapping family stress consistently, in order to target services more accurately.

There has also been innovative work to manage child protection cases using specific family support services, which is yet to be reported. If the experience of other authorities (as reported in Joint Reviews) is a guide, Garden City needs to improve its information base and application of eligibility criteria if it is not to face mounting pressure on its services.

CHILDREN IN NEED IN INNER CITY

A Joint Review, conducted by the Social Services Inspectorate and the Audit Commission in 1997, concluded that many people in Inner City Borough were 'well served' by their Social Services, adding that 'further progress needs to be made in shaping services that engage with local needs'. Social work with children mainly took the form of short episodes of involvement on duty, particularly enquiries in relation to child protection, and according to the Review, 'the demands of this work continue to put some strains on the authority's capacity to sustain other work with children in need'.

The project we researched is referred to by name as an 'excellent targeted service for intensive family support in partnership with NSPCC, with a particular focus on meeting the needs of Black children and their families'. The review suggests that more community-based services of this kind could 'act as a link (from more formal methods of intervention) 'to the wealth of informal care, community leadership and local resources'.

In the 2000–2002 MAP, some 3000 children in need were identified as being in contact with Social Services in early 2000, about 8% of the under-18 population of 37,000 (a proportion five times greater than that in Garden City). This included 340 children accommodated by the local authority and 145 on the child protection register.

The authority is very frank about the limitations of its data on need:

> those (families) who directly access services commissioned in the independent sector are not recorded. Therefore, there is no comprehensive system for establishing and monitoring the number of children in need... the information systems (that are) in place record ethnic origin (but) this information is not always available. (MAP, 2000–2002)

Both the child population of Inner City and proportions of children receiving mental health services and services for children with a disability are projected to increase. Numbers of children on the register, looked after and adopted, are projected to reduce marginally but this appears somewhat optimistic against the overall trend. Most social services' MAPs have similar accounts of steady pressure of demand against reduced budgets. Central government initiatives provide some localised relief in terms of funding, but often place higher expectations on systems that are out of date and/or depleted.

The demographic data on Inner City display the problems associated with setting and holding to a threshold for need where a substantial minority, or even the majority of children, face severe deprivation and its associated risks. Inner City authority identifies familiar groupings within the Children Act definition of need, including children on the register or looked after, children with a disability, those affected by HIV/AIDS, children at risk of offending, and children of asylum seekers. Like most authorities, they are committed to 'take account of the degree of risk and urgency and, wherever possible, draw on universally accessible services, or specific family support services rather than care outside the home' and say that 'particular attention should be given to families from Black and ethnic minority communities who often find it difficult to access services'.

Children in Need of Protection

The Child Protection register has grown from a low base of 119 registrations in 1997 to 146 registrations in 1998. The profile of the child protection register is of interest. The largest single registration category is neglect (49%) and when registrations that use more than one category are included, neglect accounts for the majority of children on the register. Neglect has traditionally been associated with deprivation and poverty, and this high proportion needs further investigation. Relatively small numbers of children are registered for physical or sexual abuse.

Approximately one fifth of registered children are known to be from ethnic minorities. This appears to be an under-representation, but may result from lack of accurate data on ethnicity. Of the 3177 children known to be in need and in receipt of services in January 2000, nearly a third of the total either raised concerns about abuse or neglect (431) or had acute family stress (517). Forty-two per cent were from ethnic minorities.

In Inner City, preventive social work appears to be directed effectively towards reducing risk in those families where child protection concerns have been raised, and keeping children off the register. As the Audit Commission points out, the price for this effectiveness appears to be that social workers are engaged in non-stop crisis work with families.

Children from Ethnic Minorities

Approximately one third of children in the borough are from ethnic minority groups. This proportion increases as children progress through the 'social services' systems, with 42% of children in need, 46% of children looked after and over 50% of children placed for adoption from these groups. These are fuller data than are available in most other authorities whose MAPs we have seen. They suggest the possibility that preventive measures at each level are progressively less available to, and/or effective with, children and families from Black and ethnic minorities as they progress from the community through the looked-after system.

If accommodation itself provided successful family support for Black and ethnic minority families, we would expect to see the proportion of children returning home increase as against adoptions from these families, and adoptions would be more representative of the local population. Unfortunately, Management Action Plans are not required to report what proportion of children who become accommodated and/or permanently separated from their families, has already received preventive services and/or has been on child protection registers.

Summary: The Local Authority's Response to Children in Need in Inner City

Inner City authority has responded to need with a traditional social work service, strengthened by family centres, youth services, and its own residential and foster carers. It has enjoyed a good reputation and adequate staffing levels. However, the current unprecedented pressure on staffing social services has meant that case work alone cannot contain referrals of children in need as well as work on child protection and children who are accommodated. Inner City is considering more innovative use of preventive resources, possibly deploying family centre staff across the whole authority or using additional mental health services as part of multi-agency family support teams.

CHILDREN IN NEED IN METROPOLITAN OUTSKIRTS

Measures of family need and stress are readily accessible, provided in the County's Children's Plan 1997–2000 and broken down consistently across eight geographical areas. This is one of a handful of authorities in England whose information base has been sufficiently developed to contribute to national data collection on children in need (Department of Health, 2001), using numbers of free school meals, looked-after children, unemployment, child protection referrals and other indices (see Figure 8.4). Outside the two urban areas in the county, which have become unitary authorities, Metropolitan Outskirts rates highest on these measures, and numbers are concentrated in very small areas. The plan recognises the existence of 'communities where there are high levels of stress on families' covering 18% of the county, and in the relevant areas, seeks to develop 'local multi-agency action plans' in 'two or three selected sites'.

The main emphasis is on children 'whose needs require a response from a number of agencies'. The Children Act definition of need is interpreted, and its duties qualified, via a stringent priority system: 'services will not automatically be provided for all children who may be described as being "in need"'. The local authority will respond, but cannot guarantee a service, even in cases where there are 'concerns that child's primary physical, emotional, behavioural and intellectual needs are not being met'. This authority is willing to risk a legal challenge to its threshold for services in order to control demand.

There are approximately a quarter of a million children and young people under 18 in the county. Those not within the ethnic group 'White' make up 1% of the population in small, diverse ethnic minority groups. The Family Stress data referred to earlier indicate that the NSPCC's Metropolitan Outskirts project falls within the third highest need area out of eight in the county. Within that area are neighbourhoods of even more intense need equal to the highest in the county, in one of which the project is located.

The Children's Plan indicates that, across the county, 17,000 referrals of need were received by social services in 1996–1997, of which 15% were related to child protection. The Plan does not give a number for children in need but since many referrals are repeats, this number (17,000) is well under 6% of the child population by the authority's definition. The county's eligibility criteria are applied to children and families as follows:

Category A—Collapsed
Children who are suffering, or who have suffered, significant harm, or who are likely to suffer significant harm.

Category B—Critical
Where identifiable factors exist indicating considerable deterioration is likely without intervention, and this may result in unacceptable risks to the child. This may also include unacceptable pressure on the carers.

Category C—Compromised
Children where there is serious concern about their health and development.

Category D—Compensatory
Where the child's disability requires sustaining and/or enhanced services, lack of which may result in significant pressure on the carer. Where there is need to intervene, to establish a more acceptable standard of care.

Category E—Promotional
Where there is a request for intervention to minimise the effect on disabled children of their disabilities . . . to improve or enhance the quality of life.

Only the first three categories attract an 'assured response', otherwise it is 'dependent on assessment of need, resources, etc.', even though the two categories 'compensatory' and 'promotional' also fall squarely within Part III of the Children Act 1989.

The authority says in its Children's Plan that 'the process through which children's needs will be determined will be by a proper and thorough assessment by its staff in each individual case, leading to a measure of priority'. At the same time, the degree of that assessment is determined by a prior appraisal, and 'the nature of the assessment process will be guided by the level of need'. The quality of first contact with families is thus critical. Assessment itself is a valuable resource, entitlement to which involves prior judgement and categorisation of need relative to other cases.

The county's Quality Protects Management Action Plan for 2000–2001 is incomplete in terms of data on children in need. The reason given is that there is a joint planning process for this population who 'require much broader responses than Children's Services alone'. Key strategic areas are developing services for children with disabilities, families under stress (as identified demographically), vulnerable teenagers, and information for looked-after children. In answer to the question 'where and why have you fallen short of expectations?' the Plan states that

> the proliferation of central government initiatives, each in themselves valuable, but not apparently coordinated or prioritised, has led to much confusion and dissipation of scarce management time across agencies. This is delaying effective implementation.

Children in Need of Protection

The ACPC Report for 1999 indicates that even though the number of children registered has risen in recent years to over 300, it is still relatively low. Physical and sexual abuse accounted for just 6% and 5% of registrations, respectively, very small numbers, which, as in Inner City, merit further examination. Unusually, apprehended or 'likely' harm accounted for 40% of registrations, with neglect and emotional harm accounting for a further 40% and 5%, respectively. This may be relevant in the light of the ACPC's focus on domestic violence and the associated risks to children. An initiative across the county had produced, and made widely available, a directory of services for victims of violence, with guidelines drawn up by the relevant services. Unfortunately, neither child protection data nor Quality Protects data are required to indicate associated levels of domestic violence, but it is likely to account for a proportion of cases of 'apprehended harm' to children.

The number of these cases in Metropolitan Outskirts suggests that they may have been registered in order to plan preventive work with their families. This could also explain the high level of turnover on the Child Protection Register, with only 13% of children remaining for over 12 months. The NSPCC project area had the second highest level of child protection registration in the county in 1997–1998, but the level has stabilised more recently. That area now has a high level of child protection referrals to social services but a relatively low level of registration. This is a feature of other NSPCC project areas in this study (e.g. Sea Side, p. 127) that supports stakeholders' accounts of successful joint preventive activity and merits further investigation.

Summary: The Local Authority's Response to Children in Need in Metropolitan Outskirts

The project areas for Metropolitan Outskirts and Metropolitan Suburbs have similar demographic profiles of high need. However, Metropolitan Suburbs is a city council committed to universal services and Metropolitan Outskirts is part of a county council committed for the past two decades to efficiency in public services. Social services in Metropolitan Outskirts have developed high quality information systems in order to target scarce resources as effectively as possible, and have contributed to central government's belated development of measures for children in need. Stiff eligibility criteria, while open to challenge, at least offer a consistent (high) threshold for the public and referring agencies and allow staff to focus on identified need. Good quality information and clear thresholds both appear critical to a managed response to demand. This in turn offers the potential for including preventive services within the response to particular types of need.

This strategic and managed response to need has gained favourable reports from central government. It is a target-led rather than a needs-led approach that at least allows some of the most pressing needs to be appraised and, with the benefit of good quality information, responded to with consistency. However, there is some evidence of understatement of need, particularly in terms of significant harm, and levels of registration may prove difficult to hold down.

CHILDREN IN NEED IN NEW ESTATE

The south-eastern county in which New Estate is located, covers a large well-populated area rather like Metropolitan Outskirts county council, with over a quarter of a million under 18s (298, 847 in 2000–2001, of whom approximately 2.4% were classified as children in need). There are seven social services areas in the county and, of under 18s, the largest group (55,941) is in the social services area for New Estate. Across the county, apart from in its two cities,

Table 9.4   Reasons for referral to Social Services (County Council for New Estate)

Problem presented	1991–1992	1995–1996	% increase
Child protection and person at risk	5,094	7,911	55
Delinquency	2,422	6,881	184
Financial concerns	2,209	2,978	35
Social relationships	1,340	2,774	107
Accommodation needs	702	1,480	111
Emotional disturbance	811	1,280	58
Homelessness	293	672	129
Other problems include hearing or sight loss, inability to cope, physical disability (OT), illness, absconding client, social isolation	11,844	15,695	33
Total referrals	24,715	39,671	61

a high proportion (75%) of under 16s live in two-parent families, just 9% in lone-parent families and 16% in extended families. New Estate area has one of the highest percentages of owner-occupied housing in the county—generally a proxy for relative advantage. However, the immediate locality for the New Estate project is an example of local high-density public housing, some of whose occupants have previously had homes repossessed. The area is one of the highest in the county for mobility of children—partly due to HM Forces camps, but also in part due to homelessness. Data for the county in which New Estate is situated show reasons for referral to social services and their relative increase over a four-year period (see Table 9.4).

Some of the service developments for children in need include:

- 11 early years centres, mainly in education buildings, with a target of 9 more;
- 18 family centres; and
- large scale use of family group conferences.

The joint Children's Plan for 1997/2000 looks at 11 priority groups for social, education and health services in the local authority area. They are:

1. children with disabilities
2. children with mental health/emotional/behavioural problems
3. children under eight
4. looked-after children
5. young runaways
6. adoption
7. young people leaving care
8. young people and homelessness

9. family support and child protection
10. young carers
11. young people in conflict with the law.

Some of these groups, such as young runaways, homeless young people and those with emotional or behavioural problems, are considered to need a preventive strategy to intervene before or during crisis. The plan states that 'it is a fundamental, although longer term, aim . . . to focus on preventative measures applicable to all children, thereby pre-empting the possibility of them coming into the category of children in need'.

Children in Need of Protection

There has been an unpredicted increase in numbers on the child protection register, across all age groups. In 1998–1999, the county rate of registration had risen from 12.7 to 14.4 per 10,000 children under 18—still well below the England figure of 28 per 10,000. However, this figure includes variations from 8.3 per 10,000 in the most affluent part of the county, to 24.7 in the area with the highest level of children in need receiving services, much nearer to the national average.

There is a relatively high level of children being re-registered as needing a further child protection plan, at 15% of first registrations. The commentary suggests that this is linked to a relatively low number of registrations longer than two years and suggests that 'targeting of resources and departmental eligibility criteria have resulted in episodic, short-term intervention'. This is a problem similar to that faced by other social services departments in this study, for instance, Inner City. It is possible that trying to 'process' families fast to meet performance targets makes re-referral more likely. The Management Action Plan (1999) argues that more sustained preventative work should counter this tendency. Social Services audited its front-line protection services, the MAP states,

to determine that services were safely protecting children. Remedial action was introduced to reinforce safety, and feedback from the Joint Review has confirmed that practice is sound . . . our vision is now to move to a family support, preventative approach to work with families. We are developing a systems management strategy, supported by services to avert unnecessary family breakdown. The thrust is to support and respect family life by providing support services, sharing care with families or extended families and ensuring that decision-making is clear and transparent in every case, based on evidence not ideology or dogma. In achieving a reduction in the inappropriate use of accommodation, a greater choice of placements will be available for the children who do require support away from home. A major challenge for the county is not only to achieve the change, but to ensure greater consistency and equity.

This strategy assumes that there is 'inappropriate use of accommodation', with a consequent cost reduction to be made in order to improve placement choice.

Children from Ethnic Minorities

Across the county, approximately 1.8% of under 18s are recorded as belonging to a minority ethnic group. A further 1% of the ethnic minority population lives in the two urban areas where there are Indian, Pakistani and Bangladeshi populations and in one of the county towns where there is an Afro-Caribbean population. The MAP for 1999 states that 'recording of ethnicity has been low therefore the accuracy of historical data has been questionable'.

Service Development for Children and Families in Need

An example of innovative service development intended to provide better decisions is the widespread use of family group conferences across the county. The 1997–2000 Children's Plan states that .

> £100,000 is being invested in this work. The local Area Child Protection Committee actively supports the development and practice of family group conferences, as an approach to increase the participation of children, family and the community in decision-making processes of child protection work. Family Group Conferences (FGC's) have been practised here since 1994 and have been underpinned by careful multi-agency planning and systematic research. Practice has continued to develop with approximately 120 FGCs being held in 1998/9. Research into their outcomes has been encouraging (e.g. Marsh and Crow, 1998) but the use of FGCs across the county lacks consistency. This is being addressed by the inter-agency strategy group. Following a second successful international forum on FGCs held in 1998, conferences are now being planned for use in the new areas of work including education, young carers and domestic violence.

Summary: The Local Authority's Response to Children in Need in New Estate

Like Metropolitan Outskirts, New Estate local authority has agreed criteria for prioritising need across social, education and health services. There may be variations in local interpretation, but the strategy is towards 'greater consistency and equality'. Again like Metropolitan Outskirts, the authority has a reputation for developing preventing services cumulatively, that is building on and modifying services over time, rather than abandoning or reconfiguring them completely.

The Joint Review by the Social Services Inspectorate and Audit Commission describes the local authority as having 'a distinguished record of innovation and of pioneering quality' with 'a considerable track record of inter-agency co-operation and joint service development' (Audit Commission, 1999). This includes the expansion of family group conferences into education and youth offender services. More recently the authority has brought together their child and adolescent mental health services, education support teachers and training and employment workers to form a multi-agency support service for adolescents. This service has initially focussed on reducing school exclusions and early reports are of some success in the targetted schools, with exclusions reduced by a third over the same period in the previous year.

CHILDREN IN NEED IN METROPOLITAN SUBURB

The Children's Plan 1997 for the City Council that includes Metropolitan Suburb is one of the few we have seen to state that

> poverty lies at the root of many problems faced by children and families in the city, particularly for those coping with other disadvantages. These make it even more difficult for families to cope with particular needs such as disability, mental health or behavioural problems.

The Plan presents eligibility criteria for children and family services as follows:

Priority One: Children potentially at risk of significant harm
Priority Two: Children whose care arrangements are vulnerable and require support
Priority Three: Children being looked after by the local authority
Priority Four: Other children for whom the local authority has a specific responsibility
Priority Five: Requests for support that do not fall into the above categories.

It is unusual for children requiring support in the community to be given priority above children already accommodated by the local authority.

The Quality Protects Management Action Plan for 1999 shows that there were approximately 8000 referrals of children in need to social services in the year 1997–1998, over 10% of the child population of the city, an even higher proportion than in Inner City. However, the authority does not distinguish the number of children in need of a service from the number of referrals. The introduction to the MAP states that there is currently no means of quantifying need in terms of numbers of children. Double counting will be difficult to avoid... we have to assume that numbers referred... only partially reflect the number whose families are unable to meet their needs.

One major problem is the lack of 'agreement with the local health authority, police authority or other agencies about the interpretation of "children in need"... there is currently no joint inter-agency definition of disability'. Poor strategic planning of family support across the city is acknowledged, including lack of consistent data that inhibits its development and the current concentration of resources on investigating harm.

No data is provided on the MAP for the key preventive Performance Indicator, 'children in need gain maximum life chances,' and there is no explanation for this gap. School attainment of children looked after for over one year is poor, with only 45% of seven-year-olds achieving Level 2 in reading, 40% of eleven-year-olds achieving Level 4 and just 15% of fourteen-year-olds achieving Level 5. No future targets for 2000, 2001 or 2002 have been set (at the time of writing) to improve these results.

A Joint (Social Services and Audit Commission) Review came to the grave conclusion that 'management had failed to ensure that practice with children and families was safe, efficient or effective, or to adequately support and develop front-line staff'.

There seems to be a greater degree of inter-agency planning at neighbourhood level than across the authority. The local Area Plan for Metropolitan Suburb includes the NSPCC as a key partner with other local agencies, and has joint targets, including:

- improving parent education and parenting skills,
- exploring new childcare initiatives,
- supporting families new to the area,
- reducing child accidents,
- developing a local family forum,
- confirming local health priorities, and
- supporting parents who have special needs.

There is pressing need for better authority-wide information management and coordination, to ensure a strategic response to need. For instance, the 1997 Children's Plan states that 'the wards which have the highest deprivation scores are also the wards with the highest numbers of Black and ethnic minority residents. However... over time, there have been fewer Black children looked after by the local authority than one might expect'. It seems that preventative services have been patchy in their response to the needs of Black and ethnic minority families. The 1997 Plan states an intention to 'strengthen and unify our approach'.

Children from Ethnic Minorities

The Management Action Plan 1999 gives the proportion of children in need who are from ethnic minorities as approximately 9% or just over 700. About half are of mixed heritage and the rest divide about equally between families of Asian and Afro-Caribbean background. A further 11%, approximately 880, are of 'unknown' ethnic or cultural background. Projections for 1999–2002 are 'not possible'. It appears that data collection in this area has not improved since the 1997 Plan. ACPC data show 15% of children registered in 1998–1999 as in need of protection falling in these groups, of whom over half are of dual White and African-Caribbean heritage. These figures are some of the very few available from Metropolitan Suburb on ethnic minority children and the City's services; if they are available in relation to child protection, they should be available in other areas of children's services as well. The MAP sets out plans for improvement including 'systems to collect statistics in the above list which are currently not available' and to 'reach agreement with other agencies about the local interpretation of children in need (and) how to count these children and (proxy indicators)'.

Children in Need of Protection

The Management Action Plan for 2000–2001 indicates that, at the beginning of 1999, over 800 children were being looked after by the City Council and over 400 were on its Child Protection Register. Reductions are planned over the next two years. Numbers of children in the city and of children in need have not been identified in the Plan, making comparison difficult. The ACPC Annual Report for 1998–1999 describes a critical SSI inspection of the City's child-protection services, which led to a review of ACPC procedures and their implementation. There were also four Part-8 reviews on children who had recently suffered severe injury or died in suspicious circumstances. By August 1999, numbers on the register had reduced to 335, some 15% lower than the MAP target. It would be interesting to know whether there were protection plans for the children removed from the register, or whether they entered the care system. There are no multiple categories of registration, and the largest single categories are emotional harm at 31% and neglect at 26%. The first high figure is attributed to work on domestic violence and the associated identification of emotional damage to children, but this is not quantified.

Summary: The Local Authority's Response to Children in Need in Metropolitan Suburb

There are many examples of good local partnership work to support families and prevent harm in Metropolitan Suburb. However, because of the very high levels of social economic deprivation in parts of the city, a tightly co-ordinated and monitored, city-wide strategy is indicated, and this has not been achieved. Local agencies have not agreed definitions of need. Social services' response to family difficulties appears to have been reactive, with high proportions of the child population registered as in need of protection and/or accommodated by the local authority. A symptom of the need for strategic grip is the lack of coherent data on need that would enable analysis and planning based on evidence. The Joint Review of Social Services provision in 1998 noted the 'disastrous effect' of economic decline in recent years. It concluded that 'while there are some gems of quality and innovation, there are serious problems with childcare...people increasingly can only access services if they have high needs and there is a high risk of danger to themselves or others.' The review comments 'preventative family support work becomes subsumed under the umbrella of anti-poverty work or services to children under eight (rather than all being) seen as an essential part of an integrated prevention and protection system.'

A lack of agreed eligibility criteria to filter need appears to result in more and more crisis referrals and a dilution of risk and need assessment. This may be a contributory factor to child deaths, and the negative cycle of ad-verse criticism and low morale reported in this local authority, an illustra-tion of the 'negative social momentum' described by Garbarino and Kostelny (1992) (see p. 64). However, it is of interest that smaller areas within such au-thorities can reverse the trend. The ward for the NSPCC project had reported a reduction in child protection registrations, attributed to good local inter-agency relationships, and public consultation that led to community support for preventative enterprises.

In terms of performance and presentation, social services are learning that there is little sympathy for attempts to maintain near-universal access, if this leads to systems that are unmanageable and risks to children who are suppos-edly being monitored and protected. Some would rather face the possibility of legal challenge from families deemed not 'in need'.

CHILDREN IN NEED IN SEA SIDE

In this county, as in Metropolitan Suburb, there is much more hard data con-cerning children looked after and children on child protection registers than about the wider group of children in need, whose education and development may be compromised. As a result, targets for this wider group are harder to set and achieve. The county as a whole reflects the national position described elsewhere (see Chapter 10). Comparing Management Action Plans and Audit Commission reports, the authorities that have built up sound data on need are in the minority but appear to have achieved more convincing plans, and more positive service user and audit feedback.

Sea Side local authority in its MAP reports the achievement of several targets, which include:

- a reduction in numbers of children looked after with three or more placements
- a proportional increase in adoptions of children looked after
- increased de-registrations of children on the child protection register for over two years
- an increase in the proportion of children on the register whose cases are reviewed to time-scale.

The MAP also sets out areas of concern, including:

- expenditure on children in need had grown by only 2% out of a planned 7% increase
- only half of children looked after sat GCSEs and only 54% had a health assessment in the previous year.

Areas of inadequate information are:

- school exclusions
- education and training of young people looked after.

An additional area appears to be the needs and services in the Black and ethnic minority populations, although there is good quality data on the large travelling population.

Service Developments for Children and Families in Need

These include:

- multi-agency family support teams aimed at early intervention in families where there are children in need and/or emerging mental health/ behavioural problems
- opening a therapeutic unit and developing professional fostering for children with challenging behaviour
- developing improved early intervention and family support with Sure Start and On Track, to develop better coordinated parent education and training
- reducing exclusions by improved behaviour support and training; improving educational input to excluded children
- improving early years childcare and educational opportunities for potentially disadvantaged groups, such as children in isolated or mobile communities.

All these actions are relevant to the areas of concern raised by the research in 1998–2000.

Children in Need of Protection

The local ACPC reported a rise of 13% in child protection referrals in 1998–1999, to 3,675, or 10 every day of the year. There was a reduction in only one year out of the previous five, with referrals leaping by a massive 39% in 1994 and 44% in 1995. Interestingly, the rate of initial conferences was held down in three of these years but then leaped by 649 in 1998. Registrations of children as at risk of significant harm increased year on year to a high of 537 in 1999. All these figures suggest the response to negative publicity over child protection.

Other agencies in the county report a similar picture, with the police child protection unit reporting a rise in referrals by a third to 1600. The majority of these cases will also be Social Services referrals. The probation service reports a virtual crisis, with a 73% increase in workload over five years. For all agencies in the county, the same problems result. Despite new posts established through the Quality Protect initiative, staffing is at a premium, with social services moving staff from early years services to cover vacancies in intake teams. In order to control the response to need, Social Services in 1998 launched a 're-focussing exercise'. Its aim was 'to ensure that children are supported at an earlier stage by other agencies, and that only those who are most in need can be assessed and provided with services by the Social Services Department.' The new boundaries left early intervention and prevention largely beyond the department's remit. This has included withdrawing funding from some family support projects.

The county's probation service also reports a shift in work, to assessing and managing risk, usually from an office rather than home visiting. The statistics indicate a continuing rise in child protection work and a proportional increase in referrals of older children aged 5–15 years. This group has formed the largest proportion of children on the child protection register for the past nine years. Neglect is by far the fastest growing category of registration, representing over a third of all registered children at the end of March 1999.

The breakdown of data for localities shows that while the NSPCC project district had the highest proportion (26%) of the county's child protection referrals (1999 figures), it had the lowest rate of initial conferences at 10%. The majority of the children on whom conferences are held are added to the register (91% or 89 children). The county town also has a high proportion (22%) of child protection referrals, but conferences twice as many, registering a larger number. These proportions suggest varying local thresholds that may reflect the work of local family support initiatives such as NSPCC's in

managing risk outside the child protection system
ures for other NSPCC project areas, for instance Met
Metropolitan Suburbs. Using family stress indicators to
cases, as in Garden City and Metropolitan Outskirts, cou
ture of how referrals are handled differentially and what use
support agencies such as NSPCC.

Summary: The Local Authority's Response to Childre
in Need in Sea Side

The local authority covers a largely rural county. Its demography is not unlike that of Metropolitan Outskirts authority. However, its Social Services Department has been struggling with spiralling referrals of children in need and at risk, and with low morale after a series of child deaths, not unlike the situation in Metropolitan Suburbs.

The two NSPCC projects in these authorities were set up on the basis of sound local research and can produce good evidence of preventive success, such as reducing child protection registrations. But in the case of Sea Side, the local authority reduced its early intervention activity in order to focus on children already on its child protection register or accommodated, and withdrew funding from NSPCC and a number of other support projects.

SUMMARY: CHILDREN IN NEED IN THE PROJECT AREAS

- As stated in the chapter on local settings, social data on children in need and at risk appear to correlate strongly with other demographic data on economic and social disadvantage. In most local authorities, a relatively small proportion of wards produces the majority of data on disadvantage and on children in need and at risk. Some authorities have a threshold of need for the whole population near to that of the most disadvantaged wards elsewhere.
- As our comparative tables suggest, data about child protection registration is much more readily available than for other categories of need, even though collecting wider data has been a legal requirement for over a decade under the Children Act 1989. Three of the six authorities had not provided even the minimal data on children in need required for Management Action Plans. Data on ethnic and other minority groups of children in need is particularly weak. It is surprising that these shortcomings have been tolerated for so long, especially when other authorities have been able to deliver.
- The data on child protection indicates a wide variance in thresholds for registration overall and for categories of registration, between and even within

some authorities. Registration for neglect, sexual and physical abuse and 'apprehended harm' are all instances.

- The data on children in need from ethnic minorities (where available) suggests that some authorities are more successful than others in preventing children from these groups remaining accommodated and being over-represented in the group awaiting permanency. Given the government's current emphasis on speeding up adoptions from care, these inequalities need close attention and authorities undertaking successful preventative work should be better publicised, not just those achieving adoption targets.

- The available data suggests that referrals of children in need have continued to rise over the last three years. Number of children registered and accommodated have until recently been held down, but are also now rising nationally. All the authorities had aspirations to offer family support via local agencies, and most had achieved this in some neighbourhoods, but only one authority out of the six had an explicit strategy to deploy preventive resources on the basis of consistent measures of relative need. On the other hand, most authorities applied more or less stringent eligibility criteria to filter out all but the neediest families from direct social work and even from assessment. In some cases, these criteria appeared to flout Children Act definitions of need, and guidance on its interpretation. Authorities using neither of these approaches (i.e. eligibility criteria or a preventive strategy based on data collection) were in difficulty. High levels of child protection activity did not appear to prevent children remaining at risk; there was a crisis orientation and critical inspections had affected staff morale.

- Some local authorities had evaluated initiatives and appeared to be achieving preventative success. These included:
  — multi-agency use of family group conferences;
  — early intervention teams including social workers and child and adolescent mental health workers, targetted on particular populations of need, such as children at risk of exclusion from school;
  — parent advice and support in schools;
  — community-based work with parents offering access to therapy; and
  — victim support for adults and children.

10

FAMILY SUPPORT NOW

This, the final, chapter looks at the context of support for children and families in need beyond the NSPCC. We describe the expansion of family support services in England and Wales, and their evaluation in targeted programmes under the present New Labour administration. We then discuss underlying issues, some of which we believe have remained unresolved for decades. These issues, we believe, must be confronted if best use is to be made of the considerable assets, in terms of resources, commitment and skills, represented by services for children and families, whether in community groups, voluntary organisations or local and health authorities. We look at the recent history of family support for a better understanding of current dilemmas, and end the book with specific proposals for the development of high quality family support.

Current issues to be addressed include:

- Uneven provision of key services for children and families, for example, child and adolescent mental health services. We found inconsistent access to key services for children and families, particularly community-based health and mental health services (see Chapters 3 and 4).
- Lack of clear (or, in some cases, any) connections between family support and specialised, referral-only services. We found that the process of self-referral or being referred to a specialist service (e.g., a psychiatrist, psychologist or social worker) was often inconsistent, unclear or user-unfriendly. It was exceptional to find feedback to families as to what was happening to the referral—families often waited in a sort of limbo. Delay appeared to be a rationing device and its undermining effect on families insufficiently acknowledged. Many parents were deterred from seeking help, or multiple referrals were made in an effort to get a response. Where family support services had direct access to specialist resources on a sessional basis, the referral process was better understood. There is a need for wider publicity and shared learning about supported experiments in new configurations of early intervention and crisis services, such as those described in Chapter 8.

- Lack of learning opportunities, confidence and status for many front-line providers and first-line managers, contributing to burnout and high staff turnover. This was most obvious in local authorities, where most of those we spoke to thought that the risks inherent in child protection work were becoming too high in relation to the rewards. Voluntary sector staff, including the NSPCC's, whom we interviewed displayed more confidence. There is an urgent need for investment and creativity in staff recruitment and retention, including use of joint appointments, secondments and sabbaticals.
- Mixed messages on the value of social work in prevention and early intervention with children in need and their families. Health, education and social work staff we interviewed saw local authorities measuring success largely in terms of work under Part IV of the Children Act with children already accommodated or in need of protection, and their adoption work, rather than in terms of their efforts to prevent these needs arising. With some exceptions, workers with an interest in early intervention and prevention were frustrated by what they saw as the lower status and remuneration for family support work as somehow not 'statutory', even where the work clearly fell within Part III of the Act. This applied to both local authority and voluntary sector staff. Government programmes offered some exciting opportunities, but usually with a specific age group or for a time-limited period.
- A need for more joint public awareness raising, campaigning and/or lobbying across organisations and sectors (depending on the issue); for instance, concerning areas where children appear to be at highest risk; data gathering and research; child exploitation; children living in a culture of violence; and the nature of child welfare and protection work. Charities should explore joint service development, e.g. for parents with mental health problems.
- Lack of rigorous long-term evaluation that involves service providers and users. While the amount of research and evaluation on family support has greatly increased in the United Kingdom, its scale is still relatively unambitious. The important questions for family support include
  — Which (if any) support services lead to improved developmental outcomes for children over time? Which services are most effective with which groups?
  — Do parent/child training programmes make a sustained difference to parents' and/or children's behaviour and interactions, and if so what element is most effective?
  — Do family support services help to identify children at risk of harm, and if so how can they best assist in preventing (further) harm while retaining the reported strengths of accessibility and user friendliness?

THE EXPANSION OF FAMILY SUPPORT SERVICES

The government's 'Supporting Families' initiative, cutting across education, health, social services and crime prevention, addresses concerns that 'in the past, government departments did not work closely enough to develop a joined-up family policy or coherent practical initiatives to support families' (Stationery Office, 1999). Initial steps included a number of preventive programmes, such as setting up the National Family and Parenting Institute to develop an information base on parent support, a grant programme for voluntary organisations, and a (proposed) expanded role for health visitors in dealing with early problems in the pre-school years. These measures, with investments in education and health, are reported as a high-profile 'strategy of support to families, which recognises the central role which families play in our society and takes practical steps to help and support parents and children to deal with the pressures and challenges which they face' (ibid).

Sure Start is a £540 million preventive initiative, targetted on vulnerable pre-school children to achieve the government's aim of eradicating poverty within a generation. The programme aims to deliver

- local services which work together in the interests of families and children;
- home visits for all families with new-born children;
- better access to early support;
- improved understanding of young children's developmental needs among parents; and
- improved developmental outcomes.

There are now some 250 Sure Start schemes across England and Wales with a further 200 planned in 2002, hopefully reaching up to a third of children under four who are living in poverty, and continuing to expand through proposed Children's Centres. Each Sure Start project should make a 'before' and 'after' check with parents to see if the service has met expectations, and a consistent set of measures are being applied by an overview team (see website for National Evaluation of Sure Start at www.ness.bbk.ac.uk; Department for Education and Employment [DfEE], 2001 and Tunstill et al., 2002). Examples of family support services suitable for Sure Start are provided by the DfEE. These include video home guidance, courses in handling children's behaviour and volunteer visiting; in other words, many of the services we have described as components of the NSPCC's family support. Sure Start was originally aimed at preschool children in the most disadvantaged neighbourhoods—approximately 5% of children aged three and under in England and Wales (DfEE, 1999).

Objectives for Sure Start include the measurable improvement of children's physical health, ability to learn and social and emotional development, and contributing to the eradication of child poverty within a generation—although how this last aspiration will be defined and measured, remains to be seen. The advantages of a national programme to achieve such ambitious aims are several: it has political backing at the highest government levels, as well as local multi-agency support, to achieve its targets, and it is accessible to the immediate communities in which it is used. Limitations are its non-universal coverage, its focus on the youngest children in families, and the possibility of its draining skills and expertise in early intervention away from mainstream services, in areas where such services are under the severest pressure.

In response to the need for a 'bridging' service to reach older vulnerable children, the government has set up 'On Track', as part of its crime-reduction programme. The programme is aimed at children between the ages of 4 and 12 who are thought to be at risk of developing criminal behaviour. Initially up to 30 schemes are being set up to identify children at risk and to offer services that are recognisably family support, such as parent skills training, home visiting and family therapy. Evaluation aims to test the theory that a range of coordinated interventions, available at critical points through a child's early life, is much more effective than single interventions (Graham, 1998).

Finally the Connexions Service offers a 'Personal Adviser' to any adolescent between 13 and 19 years needing support, particularly in the transition from school to work. The aims are perhaps the most ambitious of all the programmes: to increase participation in learning up to age 19, to improve learning achievement at all levels of ability, to prevent the onset of disaffection and promote social inclusion, and to provide practical support to overcome family or social obstacles. Personal advisers will provide advice, guidance and support; act as advocates and as a single point of access to all specialist support services if needed; and, on top of all this, build a long-term one-to-one relationship with the young person. These are demanding specifications and it will be interesting to see how personal advisers operate, and with what degree of accessibility.

Social workers have filled many of these service gaps hitherto but social work itself is hardly referred to in government material on these programmes. In launching Sure Start, the then Secretary of State for Education spoke of wanting to do 'something that would be entirely new and innovative from the word go, to get to the core of the difficulties facing families and communities', and of one of the difficulties as 'the deep cynicism about professionalism, about government in all its guises, about agencies and departments . . . the health visitor was one of the very few professionals that people would readily turn to' (Blunkett, 1999). This view runs against the evidence which indicates that the public makes massive, and on the whole beneficial, use of statutory services (see The Children Act Now (Stationery Office, 2001), Chapters 1 and 8 and below).

Figure 10.1   The framework for the assessment of Children in Need

The government has an agenda to 'modernise' social services through performance management, focussing on improving early decision-making and on achieving specific indicators in social services for children and families. In the Performance Assessment Framework and in the Quality Protects programme they have set out multiple targets for the most far-reaching levels of intervention—children in need of protection and children accommodated by local authorities. With regard to the wider group of children in need, The Framework for the Assessment of Children in Need and their Families is the government's major contribution to social services' work (see Figure 10.1). It is intended to meet a key indicator, 'to ensure that referral and assessment processes discriminate effectively between different types of levels of need, and produce a timely service response' (Department of Health, 2000a).

The framework consists of an Initial Assessment Record, to be completed by a social worker within seven working days, and a Core Assessment Record, to be completed within 35 days, including any initial enquiries about possible significant harm and a child protection conference if needed. The framework comprises 'three inter-related systems or domains, each of which has a number of critical dimensions'.

If all, or most, of the dimensions are covered, it is intended that the conclusion of an assessment should result in:

- an analysis of the needs of the child and the parenting capacity to respond appropriately to those needs within their family context;

- identification of whether, and if so where, intervention will be required to secure the well-being of the child or young person; and
- a realistic plan of action (including services to be provided), detailing who has responsibility for action, a timetable and a process for review (Department of Health, 2000a).

Clearly crucial is the pre-assessment decision as to which families receive a short or long assessment, and which families are identified as either not in need at all, or referred on without formal interview. Many of the families we met, as the framework was being introduced, were waiting for a specialised assessment, and it will be interesting to see if the framework speeds up the process for them. The framework has the potential to give greater consistency and rigour to local authority dealings with families and children in need.

Quality Protects is widely interpreted as a message that local authorities' 'core business' is with children already in need of protection and looked after, and that prevention is the stuff of centrally led government initiatives; on the other hand, the Children Act Part III gives social services a legal mandate for early intervention with children and families in need, backed by research and audit findings (Audit Commission, 1994; Stationery Office, 1995; Department of Health, 1996). By emphasising hard-end targets for children protected, accommodated and adopted, central government may, intentionally or otherwise, be limiting perception of local government to the policing role in families and thus reducing its wider relevance to communities. This is unfortunate because the quality of their community links is relevant to the government's strategy:

> the strength of the partnership between local parents and agencies at the heart of Sure Start programmes will be key to their success. Unless statutory agencies are 'levered in', Sure Start's aim of reshaping mainstream services to reach the two-thirds of young children in poverty not covered by the programme cannot be achieved. Community participation takes much longer than we anticipated and . . . depends very much on what relationships were like before Sure Start arrived'. (National Director of Sure Start, quoted in Community Care, 2001)

Social services carry the bulk of responsibility for acknowledging, assessing and at least in the initial stages addressing the needs of families who are under acute stress—those we describe as vulnerable due to their circumstances and/or facing particular risks. Referrals from Sure Start projects to social services are heavy in some areas and there is concern that

> unless the government increases funding to mainstream services, the gains Sure Start has made will be threatened. Sure Start funds tail off after next year when in theory the newly reshaped statutory services will have absorbed and rolled out the programme to all young children. (Community Care, 2001)

In 1995, a third of a million children in need were estimated to come to the attention of English social services departments annually, of which 160,000, that is about 650 every working day of the year, were referred because of concerns about possible harm (Stationery Office, 1995). At any one time approximately 32,000 are registered as at risk of significant harm and in need of a child protection plan, and there is turnover of approximately a third of children on registers each year (Department of Health, 2000c). A key social worker is responsible for the effectiveness of the protection plan for each child registered, and for coordinating several agencies' contributions to that end.

A recent survey of social services' activity in a single week by the Department of Health (2001) suggests that a huge number, approximately 400,000 cases, of children in need are being dealt with by social services. Of these, approximately 59,000 children are looked after. Over half of these, and over a quarter (28%) of the remaining 341,00 children in need (that is, approximately 115,000 in all) are involved with social services because of concerns about possible abuse or neglect, over a period of just one week. The 2003 data from the one-week survey indicate a reduction in numbers of children assessed as in need, but a higher proportion (35%) in need because of concern about abuse or neglect, as were over half (55%) of children who were looked after; in the given week, 41% of all expenditure on children in need addressed these concerns, the highest of any category (Office of National Statistics and DfES, 2004).

Even if a proportion of these cases is static for some time, we can estimate that several million children in need are in contact with local authorities annually, representing a massive information-processing and human relations exercise. There has been little publicity for these findings. The report concludes 'the data underscored the scale of the work within children and families units in local authorities, which had been significantly understated hitherto.' It also underscores the scale of the national data gap hitherto.

Failures of risk assessment and decision-making by social services rightly hit the headlines from time to time. Nevertheless, the context needs to be more accurately represented, if these failures are to be understood and corrected other than superficially. This includes appraisal of the skills gap, the number of assessments undertaken, the lack of predictive indicators for harm, and the high thresholds being applied to select those who will receive sustained help, so that in most open cases substantial risks are being managed. The Children Act 1989 did not noticeably improve on the lack of reliable data on need, particularly in very deprived areas, from which to plan safer and more effective responses. The Children in Need survey is a welcome development, but over the past decade social work with children and families under the Children Act has been compromised by the poverty of systems to collect data, locally and centrally, on this large identified population of vulnerable children.

Part III of the Children Act 1989 offered local government the vision and potential—but few resources to develop, across a number of different agencies, services that were:

- universally accessible, such as education, primary health care, and housing;
- available to certain populations and groups on account of their vulnerability, for example families living in areas with high accident and/or crime rates;
- available to families suffering severe stress, where there is concern about possible individual or family breakdown;
- available to families where some form of crisis has taken place; and
- available to families who have received services, and who may need assistance to move from specialised to community-based support.

We argue that this vision and potential may now have largely been diverted to centrally controlled programmes, albeit with much more realistic funding and reforms to benefits for the most disadvantaged families. These different levels of services and corresponding needs can be simplified or further stratified. These are discussed in detail by Parker (1980), Holman (1988) and Hardiker *et al.* (1991). The latter's theoretical matrix of 'levels of intervention' has been directly applied by many local authorities to assist in mapping and planning local support services to provide coverage at all levels. According to Parker,

> primary prevention is thought of as comprising those services which provide general support to families and reduce the levels of poverty, insecurity, ill-health or bad housing to which they may otherwise have been exposed. Secondary prevention is more specific. Once problems have arisen, help of various kinds may supply a remedy or at least forestall something worse . . . tertiary prevention would aim at avoiding the worst consequences of . . . care. At the very least, it would ensure that no further harm was done. (Parker, 1980)

It is important, however, *not* to see these levels as marking out an irreversible track or conveyor belt on which families are carried only in one direction. At every level, families get themselves (or are helped) out of difficulty and back to 'ordinary functioning' in 'ordinary' community networks. Our proposed definition of 'ordinary family functioning' (or 'responsible parenting') is *'that which provides for the immediate welfare of the children and sustains their reasonable health and development in the longer term'*. By extension, 'ordinary' communities (and 'responsible authorities') are those equipped to support families in doing this, and the governments' initiatives are intended to provide those very local resources in some of the neediest areas.

The problem for 'mainstream' services (this includes health and social services and to some extent education and voluntary organisations) is that the process by which families break down and become 'needier', passing through referral, assessment and specialist help, has been institutionalised by helping agencies, and services have traditionally been identified by *type and degree of problem* in order to attract funding and aid in processing large numbers of applicants for services.

However, the process of restoration to, and maintenance of, 'ordinary' functioning in the community after a crisis, and the skills and resources involved in promoting this, are not as well understood nor acknowledged. This research suggests that recovery has at least as much to do with individuals' use of personal support networks based in one or several communities, as it has to do with the nature of the particular problems. In terms of parental stress and children's behaviour, we saw that networks of family and friends appear to be fundamental to the use parents can make of more intensive support, in order to re-establish 'ordinary functioning'. If this is so, the capacity of all agencies that work with families to reinforce or temporarily replace networks of support, is also vital (see Chapter 6), since they provide a reserve of social capital that families can both contribute to and draw upon if in need.

Where children's health and development is thought to be impaired, only the quality and timeliness of assessment can reveal whether a family has the underlying capacity to restore their 'ordinary' functioning, and what kinds of support will assist parents to do this. Some families are unable to meet the child's immediate and, in some cases, their foreseeable needs. In a small minority of these cases, children are at severe risk. It can be extremely difficult to distinguish such a family, who may make efforts to present well, from a family whose capacity has been temporarily disabled by acute or chronic difficulties.

The Framework for the Assessment of Need offers a guide to the type and level of need the assessor is facing. The outcomes of an assessment rely both on the skills of the assessor *and* on the organisational environment in which it is undertaken. The key to safe and effective assessment and preventive work appears to be a combination of several elements. These include *experience* (and access to experience) in work with children and families and in joint working across the key agencies; *local knowledge*; and an adequate *range and depth, of support services*, plus *systems and structures*—for example, training, guidance, consultation—which promote quality assessment and decision-making. A degree of continuity and consistency over time are also important. Poorly planned change in any of these elements, even if made in the name of improvement, can lead to dangerous failures in communication. As we have already observed, in order to synthesise all these elements practitioners need sufficient confidence in their own practice to continue learning, and sufficient access to expertise to enable them to continue questioning their practice.

In addition, research and experience both indicate that informal networks are important for workers as well as for families. In stressful and sometimes high-risk work with families, building trust between staff members within and across agencies is as vital as between family members and staff.

Numerous studies and enquiry reports have pointed out the importance of good joint working in child protection practice (Birchall and Hallet, 1995). Working to explicit standards of professional conduct and challenging collusion in poor practice have rightly been emphasised by multiple enquiries and in recent government undertakings such as the General Social Care Council. Less has been made of the need, in human services operated under stress, for the promotion of understanding and respect between workers. Like all rules of engagement, standards, performance targets, evaluation measures, procedures, guidance, regulations and research findings are all vital but they are only as meaningful and effective as the relationships that mediate their application to front-line work.

The quality of work has to be judged, impartially, in terms of its effectiveness in delivering 'ordinary functioning' with families, as defined above. Experienced evaluators emphasise the difficulty of specifying complex outcomes, and the need to understand the *processes* of service delivery much better, before making assumptions about their effectiveness or otherwise. 'Researchers need to become involved in service development, conceptualising outcomes that have to do with how the service is defined, its principles and practice, over a specific period' (Fraser *et al.*, 1997). Knapp commented a generation ago that the evaluation community and by implication those that use its outputs

> will need to confront more directly the fact that imprecision and lack of systemisation have important roles to play in organisations providing human services. Systematic programme evaluation can tamper with networks of authority, communication and confidence which allow organisations to deliver their services in a complex environment. (Knapp, 1975)

Much more recently Glisson and Hemmelgarn (1998) reinforced this view, reporting a three-year study on the quality and outcomes of services to 250 children. They conclude somewhat unexpectedly that

> organisational climate (including low conflict, co-operation, role clarity and personalization) is the primary predictor of positive service outcomes (children's improved psychosocial functioning) and a significant predictor of service quality. In contrast, inter-organisational co-ordination had a negative effect on service quality and no effect on outcomes.

They found that quality initiatives *on their own* did not guarantee service outcomes 'because effective children's services require non-routinized, individualized service decisions that are tailored to each child'. The necessary flexibility and discretion, the ability to internalise and apply, rather than just follow, guidance, cannot flourish without a positive work climate. Additionally, 'increases in service coordination deflected caseworkers' behaviours from those activities associated with the quality criteria for the children on their caseloads'. They conclude that

> because many employees of public children's service systems experience high levels of stress, low job satisfaction, high conflict, de-personalization and burnout, the findings suggest that future research should focus on these types of problems rather that on the service configurations as the cause of poor service outcomes.

Measures of effectiveness need to acknowledge workers' knowledge of what works in specific local circumstances:

> organisations with uncertain technologies are characterised by (1) a lack of consensus about desirable and obtainable outcomes and (2) little or no confidence in causal certainty... members (of such organisations) have to rely on the mutual assumption of confidence in each others' works. Trust is more important than systematic information. Under these conditions, precise measurement is of little relevance or even threatening.

Likierman (1993) offers 20 lessons for managers introducing performance indicators, including the following:

'provide adequate safeguards for soft indicators',
'devise them with people on the ground, who must feel ownership', and
'find a means to cope with uncontrollable items and perceived injustices'.

He adds 'failure to take (the lessons) into account could mean not only a waste of managerial time and cash resources but also, potentially more serious, a distortion of managerial action'.

Tensions can arise on one hand between the need of professionals to sustain their authority and confidence when taking risky decisions in an uncertain environment, and on the other hand, the need of evaluators and managers to specify what is decided, when and how. The tension can be creative, but it becomes counterproductive if workers lose the autonomy that makes the work rewarding. We would suggest that the crisis of morale in some local authority children's services (Community Care, 2001) has much to do with ignorance of the social work task and a lack of ownership by workers themselves, of the process of defining and measuring effectiveness. The first point is made by a social services director of young professionals invited to shadow social workers in his authority. Although well-informed generally, 'before the visit... they had no idea what social workers did, other than that they were often connected with child deaths' (The Guardian, 2001). Clearly this is a massive public relations failure. Reviewing the Best Value regime, lack of staff ownership has been identified as a problem area for many authorities. A key factor differentiating councils believed to be able to 'drive improvement' from those who are drifting, is evidence of staff engagement and commitment (Audit Commission, 2001).

A MANDATE FOR PREVENTION? SOCIAL SERVICES DEPARTMENTS

We can see evidence of piecemeal development of family support and preventative services from the inception of social services departments. Our first historical illustration is the Report on Local Authority and Allied Personal Social Services (HMSO, 1968). The report detailed the fragmented and inadequate provision then available for children in difficulty, and argued that 'a clear and inescapable responsibility for the social care of all children who require it, must be placed upon a particular local authority committee'. Part IV of the Report cites the 'foundations of an effective (social) service' in terms similar to those used by the current administration for its preventive initiatives:

> firstly, sound universal provision, particularly in terms of good quality social housing and early years provision; secondly, a clear preventive strategy; thirdly, adequate investment in data collection, evaluation, and research; fourthly, a strong community base for the service, in terms of collaborative work with local people and organisations; and finally, adequate staff training of a high standard.

To achieve an effective preventive service for children and families, the report argued that a spectrum of universal and specialist provision such as day care (other than nursery schools), social work in schools and hospitals, and child guidance services should come under the control of local authority social services for 'the basic reason ... that the social services department will be unable to provide an effective family service without access to such facilities'. Prescient of more recent reports (Health Advisory Service, 1995) they quote the Plowden Report as saying that 'the special contribution of the child guidance service might be in educating such staff (teachers, school doctors and health visitors) in mental health'. They also recommend a variety of experiments in joint working between general practitioners and social workers, on the basis that 'it is idle to think of an effective family service without the full participation of the doctors' (our emphasis).

Many of these crucial recommendations were not implemented, and social services' task became one of coordinating provision outside their control in order to achieve the necessary results, including protection, for children. The presence of a lead, locally accountable agency for coordinating family welfare made the uncertainties and failures of interagency working with children at risk much more transparent than previously. These failures in turn brought child abuse as an issue, and with it the NSPCC, more prominently into the headlines in the 1970s and 1980s. The NSPCC helped to highlight the lack of systems to manage and monitor risk, both locally and at a national level. The Department of Health introduced child protection registers in their current form in 1989. Local arrangements for registering children at risk had operated previously.

As with the National Health Service, resources did not keep up with increasing demand, both in terms of quantity and differentiation, for services for children in need. Understanding of particular needs was refined, for instance, in relation to disability, offending behaviour and sexual abuse. Specialist services began to be developed, often by the voluntary sector in various creative partnerships, to meet those needs. The effects on children of wider social problems such as racism, homelessness, domestic violence and substance misuse were increasingly recognised, and social services were alternately depicted as 'politically correct' or as insensitive in their attempts to address them. For instance, debates within the profession about institutional racism were regarded as fanciful, before the Macpherson Report defined the phenomenon (Macpherson, 1999).

By the mid-1980s, Holman was optimistic that despite the predominance of social case work, 'the advent of patch teams, family centres and community projects has made (services) more accessible'. He felt that, in some areas at least, the 'continuum of care' was established; it was possible to envisage 'neighbourhoods composed of residents who take upon themselves the responsibilities and power to promote a locality that cares for its own, helped by statutory services which exist for the sake of residents'. His caveat was that while voluntary organisations are often more accessible, they should not act as if they could substitute for 'statutory bodies which' (he rather optimistically wrote) 'have the resources and coverage to provide preventive services for the country as a whole' (Holman, 1988).

A MANDATE FOR FAMILY SUPPORT? THE CHILDREN ACT 1989

Our second illustration of inconsistency of service development for children and families in need is the implementation of the Children Act 1989. The Act appeared to reinforce the Seebohm vision of better integrated provision by:

- bringing together public and private areas of the law concerning children and families so that there would no longer be a multi-tiered legal system and matters in court concerning families and child care could be dealt with together;
- bringing together responsibilities for children in the community, including children at risk, and those needing accommodation, so that there was a continuum of provision, rather than a set of disconnected systems;

- making local authority accommodation for children more accessible to enter, and easier to leave, so that its stigma was reduced and it could be used preventively, and
- ensuring a better, coordinated (joined up) service for children by widening responsibility for provision across the public and voluntary sector and requiring local authorities to work corporately and consult other providers.

The purpose of a full continuum of services was to ensure that support services were readily offered to children and families in need to avoid unnecessary and costly interventions. If and when circumstances demanded separation of children from their families, support services would still be available in order to restore full parental responsibility as quickly as possible.

A survey of the implementation of S.17 of the Children Act took place through postal questionnaires to all English local authorities in 1992–1993 (Aldgate and Tunstill, 1993) and was later followed up (Tunstill and McBeath, 1995). The survey indicated that social services were taking the lead in consulting other departments and agencies, but with less than clear aims at that stage, and that collaborative provision was developing, especially with the voluntary sector. However, local data collection was poor and central government did not collate figures on categories of need as they did for children accommodated or on child protection registers. Most worrying, the definition of need was both narrow and somewhat circular; 'highest priority was given to children already being looked after or involved in child protection—below the highest priorities, authorities had generally failed to define need in precise terms' (Aldgate and Tunstill, 1993). Only a quarter of local authorities surveyed defined homeless children in bed and breakfast accommodation as children in need. These findings are generally consistent with later inspections of family support, which are discussed below.

Recent studies (see Chapter 1) indicate that some provisions of the Children Act have been successfully, though inconsistently, developed. These include direct social work advice and counselling and short-term accommodation in a series of planned placements. The prerequisites identified by the Seebohm Committee—clear local preventive strategies, good universal services, readily available staff training, data collection etc., are still unevenly developed. However, the evidence reviewed for the 2004 edition of this book (see Conclusions, p. 165) suggests that the combination of an improved infrastructure and specific funding offers the first prospect of realising that vision in three decades.

THE CRISIS OF WELFARE

In the early 1990s, following the Act's implementation, long-term unemployment and youth homelessness increased, while resources for essential provisions such as affordable housing, day care and primary health care were restricted. Henderson (1995) was one of many to argue that children were

> the most obvious victims of a social crisis induced, not because the country is poor, but because it has become less equal... the facts that the proportion of children on child protection registers almost quadrupled during the 1980s and that the number of young children taken into care also increased, are as much a reflection of society's abdication of responsibilities as of government and local authority policy.

He observed that despite the legislation, social work could not sustain prevention, with 'time and energy consumed with following procedures and checking and double-checking possible abuse cases'. He made a significant observation, similar to comments on community policing following riots, that

> apart from being demoralising, to remain trapped in this framework will be self-defeating. It is untenable for (statutory) agencies to remain distanced from the lives and neighbourhoods of children and their families, especially when government funded research (Gibbons, 1992) points to positive outcomes arising from family centres and other resources.

He thought it essential to 'pull back into the policy arena, the benefits and scope of having community development and prevention as powerful components of child care and protection'. The NSPCC's Projects at Metropolitan Suburbs and Metropolitan Outskirts are examples of this philosophy in action (see Chapter 8), and we believe that it remains vital to the success of all family services, voluntary and statutory.

However, the predominance of child protection has continued; the recent survey of activity and expenditure on children in need (Department of Health, 2001) indicates that about a third and half of all expenditure is now in the abuse and neglect category. It appears that by the mid-1990s most social services departments were no longer able or willing to provide a sustained community-based preventive service, except possibly in some specialist areas such as provision for children with disabilities. Cost cutting meant the reduction of access points to services in many authorities, and other family support services such as family centres being rationed through eligibility criteria. As we have seen, families received some form of assessment, small amounts of practical help and advocacy with other agencies, offered on the basis of local rules on eligibility, and where necessary, the possibility of significant harm was investigated. The Children Act requires some family support services, such as day care, accommodation for children and family centres, to be available. However, planned short-term accommodation is readily available only to parents of children with disabilities and family centres have widely different catchment areas and eligibility rules.

CHANGING TRACK—DEALING WITH GROWTH IN DEMAND AND INEQUALITY IN PROVISION

The 'refocussing initiative' launched by the Department of Health in the mid-1990s is our third and final illustration of the profoundly ambivalent demands made on our child care system. It attempted to redress an apparent imbalance between prevention and family support, relative to costly investigation and court work, since the Children Act had been implemented. The evidence base was an audit of key community services for children and families (Audit Commission, 1994), and a review of child protection research (Department of Health, 1995). Both reached the conclusion that social services could and should develop their preventive rather than their treatment and investigation services. There were arguably inadequate resources for supervision, training, data collection or service development to make this a safe or even a realistic strategy at a time of economic stress both on families and on public services in terms of value for money.

The Audit Commission report highlighted the lack of research data on 'either the number of families needing help or the type of support required', the 'confused situation' of multiple providers of family support, and above all the uneven distribution of key preventive services, particularly primary health care. They observed:

> resources do not match need in authorities. There is little correlation between the numbers of senior and clinical medical officers (s/cmo's) and the Jarman Under Privileged area (UPA) score—a proxy for need. Similarly, there is little correlation between the numbers of school nurses or health visitors and relative deprivation as measured by unemployment rates. Indeed, work by the York Social Policy Research Unit shows that health visitor caseloads have been determined historically. (Audit Commission, 1995, Para 50)

Figure 10.2 illustrates the point, showing that the most concentrated provision of health visitors was in areas of relatively low deprivation, with around 5% unemployment. As unemployment increases, the number and concentration of health visitors actually *decreases*. As health visitors are located in GP surgeries, this also indicates that GP surgeries are inadequately distributed in areas of greatest family need.

The picture of secondary prevention via child mental health services is strikingly similar to the Audit Commission's picture of primary health care (1994).

> The survey found no evidence that, in general, the level or type of service was based on strategic planning to meet defined needs of the local population. No relationship was found between the provision of specialists and indicators of likely need such as the Jarman Index of deprivation. (Health Advisory Service, 1995)

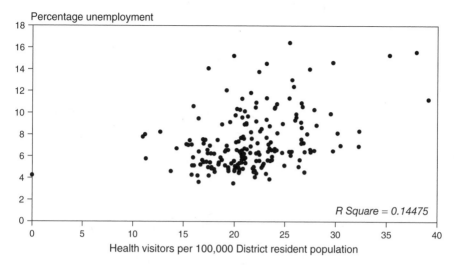

Figure 10.2   Levels of staffing related to population needs.
Source: Audit Commission, 1994

As with health visitors, Figure 10.3 shows a high concentration of child mental health specialists in areas of relatively low (though not least) depriva- tion (between 0 and −20 on the Jarman scale). In the light of such evidence, one would expect a concerted effort to attract and invite providers to work (if

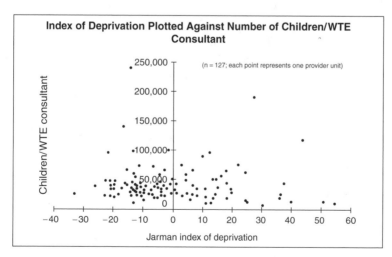

Figure 10.3   Index of deprivation plotted against number of children/WTE consultant.
Source: Health Advisory Service, 1995

not live, as in the University Settlements of a previous era) in areas of highest need. A government would be courageous indeed in attempting to direct professionals to the areas that most needed their skills. The theory of customer power spectacularly breaks down in the public sector. Market forces work for those providers who can choose a 'manageable' rather than 'hard end' supply of cases. They can thus meet their service targets rather more easily than might otherwise be the case. The same forces do *not* work for purchasers of services, and certainly not for service users, in the areas of highest need.

The Audit Commission did not recommend redistributive intervention in a health market that was apparently skewed in terms of meeting family needs for primary and secondary prevention—despite the overwhelming evidence for at least setting out the case for doing so. This was presumably considered a political non-starter. They instead suggested that primary health services be more carefully targeted via contract specification and service reviews. They failed to endorse the Cumberledge Report (Department of Health, 1993) which called for health visitors to be more evenly distributed by working to geographical patches rather than GP surgeries, despite the fact that they acknowledged patch-based work to be more helpful for interagency working in areas of high need, such as those where GPs did 'not take a keen interest in preventive work'. Indeed they reported that patch-based work was 'probably essential, where there are significant numbers of people from ethnic minorities, and health visitors require specialist knowledge of language and culture to be effective'.

Instead the Audit Commission suggested that social services' children and families departments shift priorities to meet the unremitting pressures of social need.

> Traditionally social services child care has focussed on the crisis intervention of child protection work and on children looked after. This is understandable given stringent budgets and potential tragedies if anything goes wrong. However, the Department of Health has advised social services authorities that it is unacceptable to provide little more than a reactive service engaged in crisis intervention, which effectively denies support to other children in need. Social services support is focused too narrowly at present. Prevention should be better than cure. An investment in more pro-active services should improve the possibility of reducing the need for crisis intervention. (Audit Commission, 1994, Para 48)

The profile and needs of accommodated children were not considered in the report, but the Audit Commission concluded, with some caveats, that a reduction in residential care provision for children could provide the funding. 'If all authorities were to achieve the mix of services adopted by the authorities making greater use of fostering, . . . the Commission estimates that up to £100 million might be released' (Paras 181–183). They concluded that 'in future, community health agencies will need to focus more of their scarce resources, while local authorities will need to broaden their remit to provide a wider range of initiatives that provide families with support' (Paras 181–183).

The Commission offered some creative suggestions for increasing social services coverage using help lines, universal access sites ('one-stop shops') and a broader skills-mix. But in essence they concluded that local, rather than central, taxation could somehow cover the widening gaps in provision in the most deprived areas, while continuing to manage an unknown quantity of need. This was an extremely high-risk strategy to recommend, given the acknowledged lack of accurate data on current levels of need and child protection activity, an issue that they mentioned but did not address. But it was high risk for local rather than central government.

The head of the Department of Health's Research and Development division referred to Messages from Research (Stationery Office, 1995) as 'part of a government response' to 'a series of child abuse scandals', adding that although 'no systematic information is collected about the number of children receiving (family support) services, there has been an increasing appreciation of their value and importance in recent years' (Davies, 1998). Messages from Research echoed the Audit Commission's argument that social services should 'refocus' away from specific incidents of abuse and their investigation, to earlier and broader assessment of family needs: 'too much of the work comes under the banner of child protection'. They concluded from the research that, 'excluding cases of persistent emotional harm and neglect, sexual abuse and children who have been grossly injured'

> the need of the child and family is more important than the abuse or, put another way, the general family context is more important than any abusive event within it. This message applies when defining maltreatment, designing interventions or assessing outcomes.

Of the research studies on which 'Messages' is based, very few look at long-term outcomes of abuse. The refocussing message drew heavily on a study by Gibbons *et al.* (1995), which concluded that 'there was no evidence that early injury in itself (unless it led to brain damage) caused any specific long-term harm to children'. But there are important qualifications. An injury could indicate a harmful environment, such as on-going child-rearing problems and harsh parenting style, that could produce negative long-term effects: 'parenting styles at the time of follow-up, were strongly related to children's scores on the measures of development'.

As we have seen, it is notoriously difficult to predict which families are in short-term crisis and which provide settings where a child is unlikely ever to be safe, and in most cases social workers will err on the side of caution. Underlining the difficulties of assessing parenting style, Gibbons commented that apparently harmful parenting methods, notably the use of physical punishment in a generally punitive atmosphere, were found about as often in adoptive homes as in natural families—though less often in foster homes. Foster homes are regulated and may not use physical punishment, and also have a degree of on-going supervision and support from social workers, which adoptive parents usually lack. Permanent placement in a new family, and the use of legal orders, did not appear to make a significant difference to behavioural outcomes.

There was some encouragement for planned and structured preventive input following an assessment:

> for children who remained with natural parents, packages of services that included psychiatric treatment for an adult, therapeutic attendance at a family centre and support from a voluntary agency, appear to have benefits.

The recommended combination of routine with specialist services is exactly the range of supports described in this and other studies of family support. In the light of this, it is also important to note that *where children had been registered as at risk of harm*, 'the majority of the effective service packages for children in their own home had been supported by a legal order, which possibly secured access to more resources'. These family support packages are costly, potentially much more so than a one off investigation or a permanency plan, and Messages did not come with a recommendation to increase resources.

An important additional qualification to Gibbons' report was that 'the findings refer to the mid 1980s, and patterns of service delivery have no doubt changed since then', so that 'it would not be possible to predict with confidence that the results in another sample would be the same as the ones found in this study. Thus the relationships found here could not be used to predict children's outcomes in any generalised way'. This is exactly what Messages from Research did; heavily qualified findings about practice, predating the Children Act by up to a decade, were used to attempt a policy shift in the latter half of the 1990s towards broader needs assessment and away from what were seen as forensic investigations. There was concern that joint investigations of abuse by the police and social workers using the Memorandum of Good Practice (Home Office/Department of Health, 1992) would absorb disproportionate time and resources. Although there was evidence of overuse in the early stages, joint investigations have subsequently become confined to serious cases of alleged criminal injury or neglect. Messages from Research does not describe contemporary social work activity, although useful estimates of workloads are given, and a final positive conclusion that has received little notice, then or since:

> the protection process ... seems to have some strengths. It deals with a considerable volume of work, up to 160,000 cases annually. Just over 15% of these children have to be formally registered and in 96 out of every 100 cases, children remain at home with relatives. Whatever the deficiencies, most children are protected from abuse. (HMSO, 1995)

PRESSURE OF NEEDS ASSESSMENT

Practitioners and managers in the 1990s were arguing that demand for both family support *and* child protection services was unprecedented, and that although the need for full assessments of need was understood, the skills and time to undertake them were at a premium. The first national inspection of provision for children in need under The Children Act 1989 took place from 1993 to 1995. The reality was indeed more complex than Messages from Research suggested, and a picture emerged of social services departments under siege:

> priorities were dictated by the constant demands of child protection, family breakdown and the needs of accommodated children. The balance between child protection work and services for children in need was not management driven or monitored. There was little support for front line staff in developing Section 17 work, and a danger that (they) would collapse under the sheer volume of work. (Department of Health, 1996)

Departments were applying higher thresholds in order to operate within their budgets, and facing an alarming increase in the costs of specialised accommodation for children with complex needs, for instance young people who abuse others. The relatively small number of young people involved had often been unable to obtain the therapeutic or other assistance they needed prior to reaching the threshold of being accommodated by the local authority. The introduction of community care legislation was eased by the specific grant which paid for planning and development time, whereas the lack of bridging finances to do the same for Children Act services was identified as a major reason for slow progress. Additionally, 'it was of concern that, three years following the introduction of the Children Act, management in Social Services continued to know so little about the main rationale of their existence (i.e.) their customers and their needs' (Department of Health, 1996).

Knowledge about need was not seen as empowering but as a potential threat:

> there was no incentive to understand and implement the concept (of need). Indeed, it was suggested that to identify the extent of need could lead to politically unacceptable consequences, for example public acknowledgement of the gap between needs and services, legal action. (Department of Health, Workshop Report, 1996)

Since 1997, government appears to have recognised this tension and has reversed the Audit Commission's view of 1995. For them re-focussing has meant reinforcing the tendency in many departments to concentrate on children already in the child protection and accommodation systems. But the government's long-term preventive programmes have not yet had time to

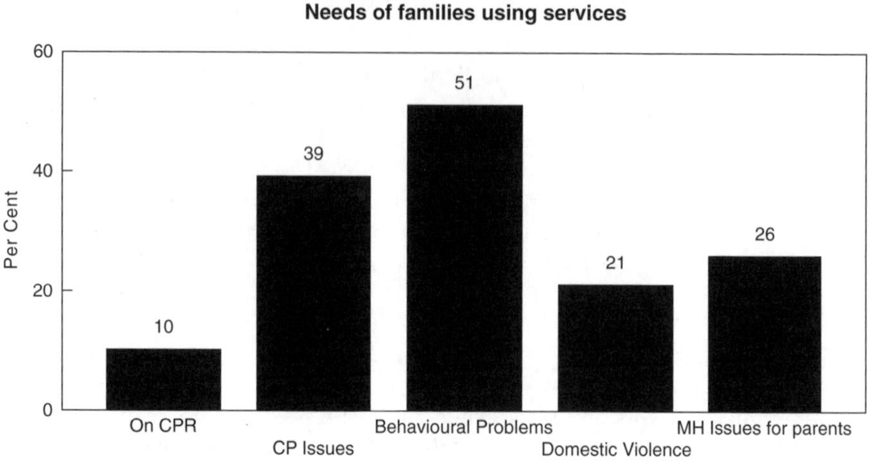

Needs of families using services

Figure 10.4   Needs of families using services.
Source: Crown copyright material is reproduced with the permission of the Controller of HMSO and the Queen's Printer for Scotland

take effect and the demand for crisis work continues, particularly in the most deprived communities, while being much more closely monitored. The result is work that is relatively high on pressure and low on variety, and widespread recruitment difficulties. Social services have not as yet benefitted from national recruitment campaigns.

There have been positive developments with regard to services for children in need, suggesting that in some areas at least the potential of Part III of the Children Act has been exploited. The second inspection of family support provided by social services, Getting Family Support Right (Department of Health, 1999), gave a more positive picture than the first. Once the need for a service had been recognised 'Social Services . . . provide a flexible, sensitive and effective response . . . almost all families expressed high levels of satisfaction'. Family centres were found to be extremely efficient, although some family support workers needed better child protection awareness. The inspection found that children's behavioural problems were the largest group (51%) of families being worked with, and that nearly 40% of children's needs related to protection from possible harm (with overlap of categories of need) (Figure 10.4).

Thirty years after the Seebohm report, concern about the waiting list for child and family mental health services remains as high as ever; 'of the people waiting for services, those waiting for child and adolescent mental health services waited longest. This did not appear to be of concern above first-line manager level'. It is also worth noting that 'a very small number of Black and minority ethnic children receive child and adolescent mental health services',—a likely result being that these children miss out on an important preventive option if they are at risk of school exclusion or of being accommodated (Department of Health, 1999).

CONCLUSIONS

The key issues and recommendations that were raised by the study in 2003 are set out below with the stage of development reached by the time this paperback edition was updated in mid-2004.

The New Labour social welfare agenda for children and families has raced ahead, revising legislation, proposing new configurations of mainstream services, and rolling out programmes of preventive support to populations in more disadvantaged communities. There has been a degree of local autonomy as to how this is done, and central government has kept a very close eye on progress, with civil servants tracking each programme. Much of this work has been done through the Department of Education and Science, which has taken over policy research and development in children and family services from the Department of Health.

For the first time on such a massive scale, local and national evaluation has been funded as an integral part of the process. The high political profile of these initiatives has at times made for tension between the relatively slow pace of local development and the centre's need for evidence of speedy improvement.

Many issues and recommendations noted in the conclusion to the first edition of this study have been addressed in some measure. Even its critics cannot argue that this government has taken a laissez-faire view of the welfare of children and families but the components of 'welfare' are still a matter of debate; they include measures to achieve improved school attainment, earning capacity, parental involvement, and ultimately the elimination of child poverty. Some of these objectives are easier to measure than others. A crucial question is how far the elimination of child abuse may be achieved through any of these measures and to what extent it is resistant to them and demands specific strategies.

Conclusion 1

More specific, preventive targets should be set in relation to the health of children and parents.

As a result of the Kennedy Inquiry (Stationery Office, 2001b), the post of National Clinical Director for Children's Services has been created within the NHS specifically to improve children's health care and well-being at every level of prevention. The post holder will chair the Children's Taskforce in the Department of Health, and oversee the development and implementation of a National Service Framework (NSF) for Children, Young People and Maternity Services. The Framework will set national standards

> that allow children to start their lives well and grow into healthy adults, ready and able to play a full part in society. It will look at prevention, care and treatment. (http://www.dh.gov.uk/assetRoot/04/08/92/21/04089221.pdf).

Each NSF is developed with the assistance of an expert reference group, including service users, carers, advocates and relevant professionals.

A review has been undertaken of the role of nurses, midwives and health visitors in relation to vulnerable children, in order to achieve maximum effectiveness (see http://www.dh.gov.uk/PublicationsAndStatistics). The recommendations include:

- improving health services for school aged children by increasing the number of school nurses; Primary Care Trusts should aim for a school nurse in every secondary school and cluster of primary schools;
- strengthening the public health role for midwives and children's nurses, including locating more midwives in community and school-based integrated teams such as Sure Start programmes and Children's Centres, additional recruitment and training including child protection training;
- recognising the important role practice nurses can play in child health; and
- prioritising the role of health visitors with children in deprived areas.

A report on innovation in Child and Adolescent Mental Health Services (Kurtz and James, 2002) indicates that multi-disciplinary services targeted at all levels of prevention have potential to improve children's engagement with education, improve their self-esteem and self-expression, and increase parental confidence. All but one of the twenty pilot projects have been sustained. However, to achieve preventive impact on a wider population of children at risk of mental ill-health would require a joint strategy of the type recommended with regard to parental support for children's learning (see below).

Conclusion 2

Social care with children and families should be oriented towards solutions, for example secure parenting, rather than continue to be defined by problem areas. There should be speedy replication of services that offer evidence of preventive success.

Conclusion 3

Open access and specialist, referred services must be developed alongside one another to provide a full spectrum of preventive services to ensure that at every level of intervention, families can be helped out of difficulty and back to ordinary functioning in ordinary community networks.

Commitment to early education and parent support has been reinforced in part due to British research (Sylva *et al.*, 2003), offering strong evidence that nursery education is the best way to close the attainment gap already evident by the age of two in toddlers from poor families.

The Sure Start programme is set to grow within 2500 new Children's Centres to be set up by 2008. Having provided part-time nursery education for three- and four-year-olds ahead of schedule, the government is now committed to provide 12,000 places for two-year-olds in 500 deprived areas, also by 2008 – the end of a possible third term of office for this administration.

These developments help achieve the government's ambitions for liberal reform:

> While the nineteenth century was distinguished by the introduction of primary education for all, and the twentieth century by the introduction of secondary education for all, so the early part of the twenty-first century should be marked by the introduction of pre-school provision for under-fives and childcare available to all. (Chancellor of the Exchequer, introducing the fourth Spending Review, July 2004)

Educational attainment is seen as the bridge to employment, social cohesion and greater equality of opportunity. The intention is that, even if huge inequalities of income and status remain, there will at least not be an underclass of children brought up in extreme economic and social poverty.

Research findings on pupil achievement and adjustment are therefore of the greatest interest to educationalists and policy makers. One key finding is that without a

> whole-community, strategic approach to parental involvement ... little return on effort can be expected. Outside this strategic approach, parental involvement activities tend to be ad-hoc, short-term and to lack follow-through. (Desforges and Abouchaar, 2003; see p. 20 for details of their Research Review).

Such an approach, they add, would need to target specific problems such as:

- extreme poverty and social chaos and threat in some neighbourhoods
- substance abuse and domestic violence
- psychosocial illness, notably depression

- the impact of a 'difficult' child
- barriers set up by schools
- inappropriate values and beliefs underlying a fatalistic view of education
- parental lack of confidence in or knowledge about how to be appropriately involved.

(Desforges and Abouchaar, 2003)

Some of these factors are known to be associated with increased risks to children's immediate welfare, as well as their longer-term development, and have been addressed by services such as those described in this study of NSPCC family support, which range from voluntary drop-in, to counselling, therapy, group work and community development.

This study indicates that where collaboration is advanced, as in Met Outskirts (see Chapter 8), evidence of greater effectiveness is accumulating. But it also found that methods of rationing the response to more acute needs are still better developed than strategies to meet those needs efficiently:

> only one authority out of the six had an explicit strategy to deploy preventive resources on the basis of consistent measures of relative need. On the other hand, most authorities applied more or less stringent eligibility criteria to filter out all but the neediest families. (p. 142, this volume).

Conclusion 4

There should be a full review of Part III of the Children Act 1989 ... In particular the success or otherwise of corporate working and cross-sector partnerships for children in need ... should be examined (and) inform joint health and social services planning.

The Green Paper, Every Child Matters (Stationery Office, 2003) and the subsequent Children Bill currently under debate (http://www.publications. parliament.uk/pa/cm200304/cmbills/144/2004144.htm), bring together the government's response to the findings of the Victoria Climbié Inquiry (the Laming Report; Stationery Office, 2003), with legal and policy developments already on the drawing board.

The Bill is intended, if enacted, to have the following effects:

1. Extend the duties of Part III of the Children Act, to safeguard children from harm and neglect and to promote their welfare, to all agencies working with families under statute, including health, police, probation and prisons. The Education Act 2002, Section 175 has already achieved this for the education sector,

but much more needs to be done to provide information, support, guidance and reassurance to assist the role of LEAs, schools and governors before concluding that it will be embraced and embedded in education practice. (Goldthorpe, 2004)

2. Outlaw chastisement that causes physical or emotional harm, while allowing family members (but not professional carers) to use physical punishment short of this. The threshold will therefore have to be established by parents themselves, by professionals who note evidence of possible harm, and ultimately by the courts.
3. Promote joint working by creating the post of Director of Children's Services with responsibility for education and children's social services, as well as by using voluntary arrangements with the NHS under section 31 of the Health Act 1999.

The Bill also promotes joint working via Local Safeguarding Boards, improved assessment and information sharing. Separately, the Children's Trust model is being piloted as a way of delivering better joined-up services for children (www.doh.gov.uk/childrenstrusts).

Conclusion 5

Specifically, the location of child care (including child protection) services should be considered, i.e. the advantages of location alongside direct services to children and parents as opposed to office-based services.

Above we drew attention to concerns that office-based services focused solely or mainly on later interventions tend to be perceived as having a policing role. They may, therefore, lose the day-to-day contact with their communities that is essential to building relationships and picking up early concerns about children at a stage before formal referral or assessment:

> Clearly crucial is the pre-assessment decision as to which families receive a short or long assessment, and which families are identified as either not in need, or referred on ... (p. 148, this volume)

The Laming Report has subsequently confirmed this view by stating unequivocally that

> It is not possible to separate the protection of children from wider support to families. Indeed, often the best protection for a child is achieved by the intervention of family support service.

It also criticises too early a distinction between children in need and children in need of protection:

> the wholly unsatisfactory practice, demonstrated so often in this Inquiry, of determining the needs of a child before an assessment has been completed, reinforces in me the belief that 'referrals' should not be labelled 'child protection' without good reason. The needs of the child and his or her family are often inseparable.

The government's response to the Laming Inquiry has included more community-based services such as Children's Centres and Extended Schools (see Chapter 1) and official guidance for all who work with children (Local Authority Circular 2003/11; see Department of Health, 2003) as to how to respond promptly and preventively when there are concerns about a child's welfare.

Other Issues to be Resolved

Concerns related to children's services include a lack of consistency in current legislation governing different services. There is also a large degree of discretion in how partnership, pooling of resources and the structure of a Trust can be interpreted, offering the potential for dangerous inconsistencies across authorities. There is concern, too, about the feasibility and cost of a national database of children and its implications for privacy and civil liberties. The lead-in for appointing Directors runs to 2008, undermining the urgency with which the Laming Report sought leadership and accountability in children's services (Goldthorpe, 2004).

Henricson (2003), among others, points out a tension in the government's wish to actively support parents, thus politicising the issue of parenting, while being seen to respect family autonomy. The result is a proactive, assertive approach to parental responsibility, in selected areas such as the punishment of parents for truancy and anti-social behaviour – with the great majority of Parenting Orders made against mothers, as being most likely to appear in court. But in other areas the approach has been more tentative and reactive to external pressures. These include physical punishment (see above), defining parenting responsibilities and rights, and the role of fathers. Sometimes it would appear that greater emphasis on 'good' child development places an enormous burden on both children and parents to achieve desired (for example, educational) results, without a commensurate interest in the mutual benefits of positive family relationships.

The Children Bill bestows parental responsibility on unmarried fathers who register their child's birth or apply to a court, but it does not specify those responsibilities in the same way as does The Scotland (Children) Act 1995 (i.e. to safeguard, direct, guide and legally represent the child as well as maintaining a personal relationship).

Tensions are inevitably created by social change such as the increasing number of children of failed marriages or partnerships, and what is described as the 'work–life balance'. Government tries to remain neutral and non-interventionist in principle; but their emphasis on non-dependency on benefit means that many young children experience substitute care for the whole working week; the quality of that care is therefore crucial. A consultation paper on parental separation (www.dfes.gov.uk/childrensneeds) attempts to balance sometimes conflicting interests by emphasising the child's needs, as well as the intention that both parents continue to play a role after separation – partly in response to protest by fathers – and the need for the courts to be fully informed of any risk of harm or domestic violence.

Having set out some of the caveats and concerns it is important to conclude by recognising that, taken in their entirety, the policy, research and practice developments described here have the potential to achieve, at last, the vision set out a generation ago by Seebohm for an effective family service (see p. 154). This would embed respect for children in communities, agencies and institutions along with the ethos of family support, and thus achieve nationally the goals this study has seen being hard-won in some localities. It would indeed be remarkable if the UK could boast a world-class synthesis of early, specialist and crisis provision and in reality, rather than in promise alone, ensure the best chance for every child.

REFERENCES

Achenbach, T.M. (1991) *Manual for the Teacher's Report Form.* Burlington, VT, University of Vermont.

Achenbach, T.M., McConaughty, S., and Howell, C. (1987) Child adolescent behavioural and emotional problems. *Psychological Bulletin* **101**(2): 213–232.

Aldgate, J. and Bradley, M. (1999) *Supporting Families Through Short Term Fostering.* London, The Stationery Office.

Aldgate, J. and Tunstill, J. (1993) *Making Sense of Section 17.* London, Stationery Office.

Audit Commission (1994) *Seen But not Heard: Co-ordinating Community Child Health and Social Services for Children in Need.* London, The Stationery Office.

Audit Commission (2001) Changing gear. Best Value annual statement.

Baldwin N. (ed.) (2000) *Protecting Children: Promoting their Rights.* London, Whiting & Birch.

Baldwin, N. and Curruthers, L. (1998) *Developing Neighbourhood Support & Child Protection Strategies.* England, Ashgate.

Barrett, H. (2002) *Parenting Programmes for Families at Risk: A Source Book.* National Family and Parenting Institute.

Bebbington, A. and Miles, J. (1989) The background of children who enter local authority care. *British Journal of Social Work* **19**: 349–369.

Bifulco, A. *et al.* (2003) The vulnerable attachment style questionnaire (VASQ): an interview based measure of attachment styles that predict depressive disorder. *Psychological Medicine* **33**: 1099–1110.

Birchall, E. and Hallett, C. (1995) *Working Together in Child Protection.* London, The Stationery Office.

Blunkett, D. (1999) Ministerial Statement.

British Medical Association (1999) *Growing Up in Britain.* BMJ Books.

Bunn, A. and Gardner, R. (forthcoming) Report of a monitoring exercise on quality parenting and family support activity. Royal Holloway College/NSPCC.

Butt, J. and Box, L. (1998) *Family Centred.* London, Race Equality Unit.

Cawson, P., Wattam, C., Brooker, S., and Kelly, G. (2000) *Child Maltreatment in the United Kingdom: A Study of the Prevalence of Child Abuse and Neglect.* London, NSPCC.

Children Bill (2004) http://www.publications.parliament.uk/pa/cm200304/cmbills/144/2004144.htm

Community Care (Oct. 2001) Children's services.

Community Care (Oct. 2001) Start right.

Community Care (Oct. 2001) System overload.

Cummings, C., Dyson, A., and Todd, L. (2004) *Evaluation of the Extended Schools Pathfinder Projects.* London: DfES Research Report RR 530.

Davies, C. (1998) Developing interests in child care outcome measurement: A central government perspective. *Children and Society* **12**: 155–160.

Department for Education and Employment (1999) *Sure Start: Making a Difference for Children and Families*. London, DfEE.

Department for Education and Employment (2001) *Sure Start: A Guide to Fourth Wave Programmes*. London, DfEE.

Department for Education and Skills (2003) The Children Act Report 2002. London, DfES.

Department of Health (1993) *Changing Childbirth. Part I: Report of the Expert Maternity Group; Part II: Survey of Good Communications Practice in Maternity Services*. London, HMSO.

Department of Health (1995) *Child Protection, Messages From Research*. London, The Stationery Office.

Department of Health (1996) *Children in Need—Report of a SSI National Inspection of Social Services Departments' Family Support Services 1993–1995*. London, The Stationery Office.

Department of Health (1999) *Getting Family Support Right*. London, The Stationery Office.

Department of Health (2000a) *Framework for the Assessment of Children in Need and their Families*. London, The Stationery Office.

Department of Health (2000b) *Not Really Child's Play*. London, The Stationery Office.

Department of Health (2000c) *Children and Young People on Child Protection Registers*. London, The Stationery Office.

Department of Health (2001) *Children in Need, a Survey of Activity and Expenditure*. London, The Stationery Office.

Department of Health. (2003) *What To Do if You're Worried a Child is Being Abused*. Local Authority Circular LAC 2003/11.

Desforges, C. and Abouchaar, A. (2003) *The Impact of Parental Involvement, Parental Support and Family Education on Pupil Achievement and Adjustment: A Literature Review*. London, DfES Research Report RR 433.

Education Act 2002 (c. 32) The Stationery Office.

Eyberg, S.M. and Matarazzo, R.G. (1980) Training parents as therapists: A comparison between individual parent–child interaction training and parent group didactic training. *Journal of Clinical Psychology* 36(2): 492–499.

Forehand, R.L., Furey, W.M., and McMahon, R.J. (1984) The role of maternal distress in a parent training program to modify child noncompliance. *Behavioural Psychotherapy* 12: 93–108.

Fraser, M.W., Nelson, K.E., and Rivard, J.C. (1997) Effectiveness of family preservation services. *Social Work Research* 21 (3): 138–153.

Frost, N., Johnson, L., Stein, M., and Wallis L. (1996) *Negotiated Friendship: Home-Start and the Delivery of Family Support*. Leeds, Leeds University.

Furstenberg, F. et al. (1999) *Managing to Make It*. Chicago, The University of Chicago Press.

Garbarino, J. and Kostelny, K. (1992) Child abuse and neglect as a community problem. *Child Abuse and Neglect* 16: 455–464.

Garbarino, J. and Sherman, D. (1980) High risk neighbourhoods and high risk families: The ecology of child maltreatment. *Child Development* 51: 188–198.

Gardner, R. (1991) *Supporting Families: Preventative Social Work in Practice*. London, National Children's Bureau.

Gardner, R. (1998) *Family Support*. Birmingham, Venture Press.

Gardner, R. (in press) *Supporting Families: A Professional Guide to Child Protection*. Chichester, England, John Wiley & Sons, Ltd.

Ghate, D. and Hazel, N. (2002) *Parenting in Poor Environments: Stress, Support and Coping*. London, Jessica Kingsley Publishers.

Gibbons, J. (1992) *The Children Act 1989 and Family Support: Principles into Practice.* HMSO.

Gibbons, J., Gallagher, B., Bell, C., and Gordon, D. (1995) *Development After Physical Abuse in Early Childhood: A Follow-Up Study of Children on Protection Registers.* Studies in child protection. London, The Stationery Office.

Gibbons, J., Thorpe, S., and Wilkinson, P. (1990) *Family Support and Prevention: Studies in Local Areas: Purposes and Organisation of Preventive Work with Families.* London, HMSO.

Gilgun, J. (1996) Relationships Among Family Members (http://160.94.100.50/faculty/jgilgun/caspars/htm).

Gill, A. (1998) *What Makes Parent Training Groups Effective?: Promoting Positive Parenting Through Collaboration.* Thesis for Doctor of Philosophy, University of Leicester.

Glisson, C. (1996) Judicial and service decisions. *Social Sciences Review* **70**: 257–281.

Glisson, C. and Hemmelgarn, A. (1998) The effects of organisational climate. *Child Abuse and Neglect* **22**(5): 401–421.

Goldthorpe, L. (2004) Every Child Matters: a legal perspective. *Child Abuse Review* **13**(2): 115–136.

Goodman, R.L. (1997) The strengths & difficulties questionnaire: A research note. *Psychology and Psychiatry* **38**(5): 581–586.

Gordon, D., Adelman, L., Ashworth, K., Bradshaw, J., Levitas, R., Middleton, S. et al. (2000) *Poverty and Social Exclusion in Britain.* York, Joseph Rowntree Foundation.

Graham, J. (1998) Promoting a less criminal society. What works in preventing criminality, in Goldblatt, P. and Lewis, C. (eds), *Reducing Offending: An Assessment of Research Evidence on Ways of Dealing With Offending Behaviour.* Home Office Research Study No. 187.

Hall, D. and Elliman, D. (eds) (2003) *Health For All Children* (4th edn). Oxford, Oxford University Press.

Hardiker, P., Exton, K., and Barker, M. (1991) The social policy contexts of prevention in child care. *British Journal of Social Work* **21**: 341–359.

Health Advisory Service (1995) *Together We Stand: Child & Adolescent Mental Health Services.* London, HMSO, p. 39.

Henderson, P. (1995) *Children and Communities.* London, England, Pluto Press.

Henricson, C. (2003) *Government and Parenting: Is There a Case For a Policy Review and a Parenting Code?* London, National Family and Parenting Institute.

Hills, J., Le Grand, J., and Piachaud, D. (eds) *Understanding Social Exclusion.* Oxford, Oxford University Press.

HMSO (1968) Report of the committee on local authority and allied personal social services (The Seebohm Report).

Holman, B. (1988). *Putting Families First.* London, Macmillan.

Home Office/Department of Health (1992) Memorandum of Good Practice on video recorded interviews with child witnesses for criminal proceedings, London, Stationery Office.

Knapp, M.S. (1975) Tampering with open systems, in Datta LE and Perloff R (eds), *Improving Evaluations.* Beverley Hills/London.

Kurtz, Z. and James, C. (2003) *What's New?: Learning From the CAMHS Innovation Projects. Summary.* London, Department of Health.

Likierman, A. (1993) Performance indicators: Twenty early lessons. *Public Money and Management*, Oct./Dec.

Macpherson, W. (1999) *The Stephen Lawrence Inquiry.* London, Home Office.

Malton, N. (2000). *A History of the NSPCC: Protecting Children From Cruelty Since 1884.* London, NSPCC.

Maluccio, A.N. (1998) Assessing child welfare outcomes: The American perspective. *Children and Society* **12**: 161–168.

Marsh, P. and Crow, G. (1998) *Family Group Conferences in Child Welfare*. Oxford, Blackwell.

NECF (2003) Developing Collaboration in Preventative Services for Children and Young People: The National Evaluation of the Children's Fund First Annual Report 2003. London, DfES Research Report RR 528.

Office of National Statistics and DfES (2004) *Children in Need in England*. London, DfES.

Parker, R.A. (1980) *Caring for Deprived Children*. London, National Children's Bureau.

Pecora, P.J., Fraser, M.W., Nelson, K.E., McCroskey, J., and Meezan, W. (1995) Evaluating family-based services, in *Modern Applications of Social Work*. Hawthorne, NY, Aldine de Gruyter.

Quinton, D. (2004) *Supporting Parents: Messages from Research*. London, Jessica Kingsley Publishers.

Report on nursing and midwifery services for children (2004) http://www.dh.gov.uk/PublicationsAndStatistics

Rix, J. (2004) Youthful Outlook. Guardian Society 24/03/04. www.SocietyGuardian. co.uk/children. M.Kellet@open.ac.uk

Social Services Inspectorate (1999) *Getting Family Support Right: Inspection of the Delivery of Family Support Services*. Department of Health.

Stationery Office (1995) Child protection: messages from research.

Stationery Office (1999) Tackling poverty and social exclusion.

Stationery Office (2001) The Children Act Now: messages from research.

Stationery Office (2001b) Learning from Bristol, the report of the public inquiry into children's heart surgery at the Bristol Royal Infirmary 1984–1995: summary and recommendations. And at http://www.bristol-inquiry.org.uk/.

Stationery Office (2003) The Victoria Climbié Inquiry: report of an inquiry by Lord Laming.

Sylva, K., Melhiush, E., Sammons, P., Siraj-Blatchford, I., Taggart, B., and Elliot, K. (2003) *The Effective Provision of Pre-school Education (EPPE) Project: Findings from the Pre-school Period*. London, Institute of Education, University of London.

The Guardian (17 Oct. 2001).

Thoburn, J., Wilding, J., and Watson, J. (2000) Family Support in Cases of Emotional Maltreatment and Neglect. London, The Stationery Office.

Tunstill, J. and Aldgate, J. (2000) Services for Children in Need. London, The Stationery Office.

Tunstill, J., Allnock, D., Meadows, P., and McLeod, A. (2002) *Early Experiences of Implementing Sure Start*. London, DfES.

Tunstill, J., Hughes, M., and Aldgate, J. (forthcoming) *Family Support at the Centre*. London, Jessica Kingsley Publishers.

Tunstill, J. and McBeath, G. (1995) *Implementation of Part 3 of The Children's Act 1989*. London, National Council for Voluntary Child Care Organizations.

Warren, C. (1997) Family support and empowerment, in Cannon, C. and Warren, C. (eds), *Social Action With Children and Families*. London, Routledge.

Wattam, C. (1997) Can filtering be rationalised? in Parton, N. (ed.), *Child Protection and Family Support*. London, Routledge.

Webster-Stratton, C. and Herbert, M. (1994) Troubled families—problem children, in *Working With Parents: A Collaborative Process*. Chichester, England, Wiley.

Whittaker, J.K. (1991) The leadership challenge in family based services: Policy, practice and research. *Families in Society: Journal of Contemporary Human Services* **72**(5): 294–300.

READING LIST

Aldgate, J. and Statham, J. (2001) *The Children Act Now: Research on the Implementation of the Children Act 1989*. London, The Stationery Office.

Aldgate, J. and Tunstill, J. (1995) *Implementing Section 17 of the Children Act 1989—the First 18 Months*. Leicester University Press/Department of Health.

Baldwin, N. and Spencer, N. (1993) Deprivation and child abuse: Implications for strategic planning in children's services. *Children and Society* **7**: 357–375.

Barter, C. (1999) *Protecting Children From Racism and Racist Abuse*. London, National Society for the Protection of Cruelty to Children.

Batty, D. and Cullen, D. (ed.) (1996) *Child Protection: The Therapeutic Option*. London, British Agencies for Adoption and Fostering.

Bebbington, A. and Miles, J. (1989) The background of children who enter local authority care. *British Journal of Social Work* **19**: 349–369.

Berrueta-Clement, J., Schweinhart, L., Barnett, W., Epstein, A., and Weikart, D. (1984) *Changed Lives: The Effects of the Perry Pre-School Program on Youths Through Age 19* (Monographs of the High/Scope Educational Research Foundation, No. 8). Ypsilanti, MI, High/Scope Press.

Birchall, E. and Hallett, C. (1995) *Working Together in Child Protection*. London, Stationery Office.

Brandon, M., Lewis, A., and Thoburn, J. (1996) The Children act definition of "significant harm" interpretation in practice. *Health and Social Care in the Community* **4**(1): 11–20.

Brandon, M., Lewis, A. Thoburn, J., and Way, A. (1999) *Safeguarding Children With the Children Act 1989*. London, Stationery Office.

Bretherton, I. and Waters, E. (ed.) (1985) *Growing Points of Attachment Theory and Research*. Monograph 209 of the Society for Research in Child Development, University of Chicago.

British Medical Association (1999) *Growing Up in Britain*. BMJ Books.

Brown, G.W., Andrews, B., Harris, T., Adler, Z., and Bridge, L. (1986) Social support, self-esteem and depression. *Psychological Medicine* **16**(4): 813–831.

Buchanan, A. (1999) *What Works for Troubled Children?* Essex, England, Barnardo's.

Butt, J. and Mirza, K. (1996) *Social Care and Black Communities: A Review of Recent Research Studies*. London, HMSO.

Cannon, C. and Warren, C. (1997) *Social Action With Children and Families*. London, Routledge.

Carter, J. (ed.) (1998) *Post Modernity and the Fragmentation of Welfare*. London, Routledge.

Cawson, P., Wattam, C., Brooker, S., and Kelly, G. (2000) *Child Maltreatment in the United Kingdom: A Study of the Prevalence of Child Abuse and Neglect*. London, National Society for the Protection of Cruelty to Children.

Cleaver, H. and Freeman, P. (1995) *Parental Perspectives in Cases of Suspected Child Abuse.* London, HMSO.

Dale, P., Davies, M., Morrison, T., and Waters, J. (1986) *Dangerous Families: Assessment and Treatment of Child Abuse.* London, Tavistock.

De Ball, D. (1999) *What Do We Know about the Effectiveness of Parenting Support Initiatives?* Norwich, England, Healthy Norfolk.

Department of Health (1991) *Outcomes in Child Placement.* London, Stationery Office.

Department of Health (1995) *Working Together to Safeguard Children.* London, Stationery Office.

Department of Health (1997) *Responding to Families in Need.* London, Stationery Office.

Department of Health (1999) *Children and Young People on Child Protection Registers.* London, Stationery Office.

Department of Health (2001) *Working Together to Safeguard Children.* London, Stationery Office.

Dingwall, R., Eekelaar, J., and Murray, T. (1983) *The Protection of Children.* Oxford, Blackwell.

Donnelly, B. (1990) *Self-Help Projects for Families and Children.* London, National Children's Bureau.

Fox Harding, L. (1991) *Perspectives in Child Care Policy.* London, Longman.

Frost, N., Johnson, L., Stein, M., and Wallis, L. (1996) *Negotiated Friendship. Home-Start and the Delivery of Family Support.* Leicester, Home-Start UK.

Gardner, R. and Manby, M. (1993) Family support. *Fostering and Adoption* 7: 3.

Gelles, R.T. (1987) *Family Evidence.* London, Sage.

Gibbons, J., Conroy, S., and Bell, C. (1995) *Operating the Child Protection System.* London, Stationery Office.

Gough, D. (1994) The literature on prevention. *Child Abuse Review* 3: 317–322.

Halsey, A.H. (1988) *Change in British Society.* Oxford, Oxford University Press.

Hardiker, P., Exton, K., and Barker, M. (1991) The social policy contexts of prevention in child care. *British Journal of Social Work* 21: 341–359.

Heiner, M. (1992) Prevention and utilisation of research, in Otto, H. and Flosser, G. (eds), *How to Organise Prevention.* Hawthrone, NY, Aldine de Gruyter.

Henderson, P. (1995) *Children and Communities.* London, England, Pluto Press.

Higgins, K., Pinkerton, J., and Davine, P. (1998) *Family Support in Northern Ireland.* The Queens University Belfast.

H.M. Treasury (1988) Cross-departmental review of provision for young children.

Hutton, W. (1995) The state we're in. Cape.

Johnson, L. (1993) *Families in Partnership.* London, Family Service Units.

Little, M. and Mount, K. (1999) *Prevention and Early Intervention With Children in Need.* England, Ashgate.

MacDonald, G. (1998) Promoting evidence-based practice in child protection. Clinical *Child Psychology and Psychiatry* 3(1): 71–85.

Macdonald, G. and Roberts, H. (1995) *What Works in the Early Years?* Essex, England, Barnardo's.

MacDonald, G. and Winkley, A. (1999) *What Works in Child Protection?* Essex, England, Barnardo's.

Madge, N. (1997) Abuse and survival: A fact file. The Prince's Trust.

Makins, V. (1997) *Not Just a Nursery.* London, National Children's Bureau.

Marsh, P. and Tresiliotis, J. (1993) *Prevention and Reunification in Child Care.* London, British Agencies for Adoption and Fostering.

McAuley, C. (1999) *The Family Support Outcomes Study.* Leicester, Home-Start UK.

Miller, W.R. and Rollnick, S. (1991) *Motivational Interviewing*. New York, Guildford Press.

NCH Action for Children (2000) Factfile 2000.

Newell, P. (1991) The UN convention and Children's Rights in the UK. The Children's Society.

NSPCC and The University of Central Lancashire (2000) Social inclusion and family support.

Open University, School of Health and Social Welfare (1997) Confident parents, confident children, in *A Study Pack Intended to Help Parents and Carers to Develop Confidence and Self Esteem*. Milton Keynes, England, Open University.

Otto, H.U. and Flosser, G. (ed.) (1992) *How to Organise Prevention*. Hawthrone, NY, Aldine de Gruyter.

Owen, H. and Pritchard, J. (1993) *Good Practice in Child Protection*. London, Jessica Kingsley.

Parker, R. (ed.), Ward, H. (ed.), Jackson, S. (ed.), Algate, J. (ed.), and Wedge, P. (ed.) (School of Applied Social Studies, University of Bristol), Department of Health (DoH) (1991) Looking after children: assessing outcomes in child care: The report of an independent working party established by the Department of Health. London, Stationery Office.

Parton, N. (1997) *Child Protection and Family Support*. London, Routledge.

Qureshi, T., Berridge, D., and Wenman, H. (2000) *Where to Turn? Family Support for South Asian Communities*. London, National Children's Bureau.

Report of the all-party parliamentary group on parenting (1999). London, The Stationery Office.

Rose, W. (1994) An overview of the development of services—the relationship between protection and family support and the intentions of the Children Act 1989, for the Sieff Conference, Department of Health.

Schaffer, H.R. (1990) *Making Decisions About Children: Psychological Questions and Answers*. Oxford, Blackwell.

Secretary of State for Social Security (1999) *Opportunity for All: Tackling Poverty and Social Exclusion*. London, The Stationery Office.

Shaw, I. and Lishman, J. (1999) *Evaluation and Social Work Practice*. London, Sage.

Smith, C. (1997) *Developing Parenting Programmes*. London, National Children's Bureau.

Social Services Inspectorate (1997) *Responding to Families in Need*. Department of Health.

Stationery Office (1996) Childhood Matters. Report of the national commission of inquiry into the prevention of child abuse.

Statistics Office (1994, 1995 and 1996) *Social Focus on Children*. London, Stationery Office.

Stone, W. and Warren, C. (1998) *Protection or Prevention?* London, National Council for Voluntary Child Care Organizations.

Thoburn, J. and Lewis, A. (1992) Partnership with parents of children in need of protection, in Gibbons, J. (ed.) *The Children Act 1989 and Family Support: Principles into Practice*. London, Stationery Office.

Thorpe, D. (1994) *Evaluating Child Protection*. Milton Keynes, England, Open University.

Tunstill, J. (1995) The Children Act and the voluntary child care sector. *Children and Society* 5: 76–86.

Tunstill, J. (1996) Family support: Past, present and future challenges. *Child and Family Social Work* 1: 151–158.

Utting, D. (ed.) (1996) Families and parenting conference report. London, Family Policy Studies Centre.

Vincenti, O. (1999) *NSPCC Services to Black and Minority Ethnic Children & Families.* London, National Society for the Protection of Cruelty to Children.

Walker, A. and Walker, C. (1987) *The Growing Divide.* London, Child Poverty Action Group.

Webster-Stratton, C. (1984) Randomized trial of two parent training programs for families with conduct disordered children. *Journal of Consulting and Clinical Psychology* **52**(4): 666–678.

Webster-Stratton, C. (1997) Treating children with early onset conduct problems: A comparison of child and parent training interventions. *Journal of Consulting and Clinical Psychology* **65**: 93–109.

Williams, K. and Gardner, R. (1996) *Caring for Children.* London, Longman.

APPENDIX (METHODOLOGY)

PARENT'S HEALTH QUESTIONNAIRE*

These are a few questions about your own health at the moment. You are asked to answer each question Yes or No.

Please ring the correct answer.

1.	Do you often have backache?	Yes	No
2.	Do you feel tired most of the time?	Yes	No
3.	Do you often feel miserable or depressed?	Yes	No
4.	Do you often have bad headaches?	Yes	No
5.	Do you often get worried about things?	Yes	No
6.	Do you usually have great difficulty in falling asleep or staying asleep?	Yes	No
7.	Do you usually wake unnecessarily early in the morning?	Yes	No
8.	Do you wear yourself out worrying about your health?	Yes	No
9.	Do you often get in a violent rage?	Yes	No
10.	Do people often annoy and irritate you?	Yes	No
11.	Have you at times had a twitching of the face, head or shoulders?	Yes	No
12.	Do you often suddenly become scared for no good reason?	Yes	No
13.	Are you scared to be alone when there are no friends near you?	Yes	No
14.	Are you easily upset or irritated?	Yes	No
15.	Are you frightened of going out alone or of meeting people?	Yes	No
16.	Are you constantly keyed up or irritated?	Yes	No
17.	Do you suffer from indigestion?	Yes	No
18.	Do you often suffer from an upset stomach?	Yes	No
19.	Is your appetite poor?	Yes	No
20.	Does every little thing get on your nerves?	Yes	No
21.	Does your heart often race like mad?	Yes	No
22.	Do you often have bad pains in your eyes?	Yes	No
23.	Are you troubled with rheumatism or fibrositis?	Yes	No
24.	Have you ever had a nervous breakdown?	Yes	No

---

* Also known as Malaise Inventory (see Gibbons *et al.*, 1990).

STRENGTHS AND DIFFICULTIES QUESTIONNAIRE
(see **Goodman, 1997**)

For each item, please mark the box for Not True, Somewhat True or Certainly True. It would help us if you answered all items as best you can even if you are not absolutely certain or the item seems daft! Please give your answers on the basis of the child's behaviour over the last six months or this school year.

Child's Name .... Male/Female

Date of Birth ....

	Not true	Somewhat true	Certainly true
Considerate of other people's feelings	☐	☐	☐
Restless, overactive, cannot stay still for long	☐	☐	☐
Often complains of headaches, stomachaches or sickness	☐	☐	☐
Shares readily with other children (treats, toys, pencils etc.)	☐	☐	☐
Often has temper tantrums or hot tempers	☐	☐	☐
Rather solitary, tends to play alone	☐	☐	☐
Generally obedient, usually does what adults request	☐	☐	☐
Many worries, often seems worried	☐	☐	☐
Helpful if someone is hurt, upset or feeling ill	☐	☐	☐
Constantly fidgeting or squirming	☐	☐	☐
Has at least one good friend	☐	☐	☐
Often fights with other children or bullies them	☐	☐	☐
Often unhappy, down-hearted or tearful	☐	☐	☐
Generally liked by other children	☐	☐	☐
Easily distracted, concentration wanders	☐	☐	☐
Nervous or clingy in new situations, easily loses confidence	☐	☐	☐
Kind to younger children	☐	☐	☐
Often lies or cheats	☐	☐	☐
Picked on or bullied by other children	☐	☐	☐
Often volunteers to help others (parents, teachers, other children)	☐	☐	☐
Thinks things out before acting	☐	☐	☐
Steals from home, school or elsewhere	☐	☐	☐
Gets on better with adults than with other children	☐	☐	☐
Many fears, easily scared	☐	☐	☐
Sees tasks through to the end, good attention span	☐	☐	☐

Do you have any other comments or concerns?

Overall, do you think that your child has difficulties in one or more of the following areas: emotions, concentration, behaviour or being able to get on with other people?

	No	Yes—minor difficulties	Yes—definite difficulties	Yes—severe difficulties
	☐	☐	☐	☐

If you have answered "Yes", please answer the following questions about these difficulties:

• How long have these difficulties been present?

Less than a month	1–5 months	6–12 months	Over a year
☐	☐	☐	☐

• Do the difficulties upset or distress your child?

Not at all	Only a little	Quite a lot	A great deal
☐	☐	☐	☐

• Do the difficulties interfere with your child's everyday life in the following areas?

	Not at all	Only a little	Quite a lot	A great deal
HOME LIFE	☐	☐	☐	☐
FRIENDSHIPS	☐	☐	☐	☐
CLASSROOM LEARNING	☐	☐	☐	☐
LEISURE ACTIVITIES	☐	☐	☐	☐

• Do the difficulties put a burden on you or the family as a whole?

Not at all	Only a little	Quite a lot	A great deal
☐	☐	☐	☐

Signature... Date...

Mother/Father/Other (Please specify):

FAMILY SUPPORT EVALUATION 1998–2000—NETWORKS OF SUPPORT (2ND VERSION)

Section One: YOUR Local Area or Neighbourhood and YOU

1.1 What do you call your local area or neighbourhood?

1.2 How do you rate the local area as one to raise children in?
Very Good   **Good**   **Neutral**   **Bad**   **Very Bad**

1.3 Is this as safe as other parts of ....?
Yes as safe   No not as safe

1.4 Do neighbours help each other out?
Often   Sometimes   Never

1.5 Do neighbours visit each others homes?
Often   Sometimes   Never

1.6 Do you feel at home in   your house/flat   **Y/neutral/N**
                                your road/block   **Y/neutral/N**
                                your estate   **Y/neutral/N**

1.7 Have residents solved a community problem?   **Y / N**

1.8 How long have you lived in your local area/neighbourhood?
Yrs.........mnths.........

1.9 How long do you expect to stay in the local area/neighbourhood?
Years.........mnths.........

1.10 **Commentary:**

Section Two: YOUR Networks of Support

2.1 Please indicate which are **Supportive** and/or **Difficult** relationships by
S and/or **D** (some may be the same people):

Informal	A little	Very
Partner	S/D	S/D
Child	S/D	S/D
Friend	S/D	S/D
Neighbour	S/D	S/D
Relative	S/D	S/D
Other	S/D	S/D

Commentary:

2.2 How near is the most supportive of these?
1/2 m   1 m   over 2 m

2.3 Does s/he offer support to you as an Individual **(I)** and/or Parent **(P)** and/or Community Resident **(CR)**?

I   P   CR

2.4 (See 2.1 for guidance)

Semiformal	A little	Very
Volunteer	S/D	S/D
Group	S/D	S/D
Club	S/D	S/D
Church	S/D	S/D
Class	S/D	S/D
Other	S/D	S/D

Commentary:

2.5 How near is the most supportive of these?

1/2 m   1 m   over 2 m

2.6 Does s/he offer support to you as an Individual **(I)** and/or a Parent **(P)** and/or a Community Resident **(CR)**?

I   P   CR

2.7

Formal	A little	Very
Doctor	S/D	S/D
Solicitor	S/D	S/D
Social Worker	S/D	S/D
Health Visitor	S/D	S/D
Solicitor	S/D	S/D
Other	S/D	S/D

2.8 How near is the most supportive of these?

1/2 m   1 m   over 2 m

2.9 Does s/he offer support to you as an Individual **(I)** and/or a Parent **(P)** and/or a Community Resident **(CR)**?

I   P   CR

Section Three: The Project

3.1 Do you know which organisations run the project?   Y / N
Name 1............................   Name 2............................

3.2 Is the fact that NSPCC is one
A bad thing   Neutral   A good thing

3.3 And Why?

3.4 How did you come to the project?
On my own—no one else involved
A friend/neighbour/relative assisted
A volunteer or informal helper assisted
A professional assisted/referred
Other

3.5 How long have you used the project?   **Yrs.......... Mnths.........**

3.6 What services have you received?
For yourself ....

For a child ....

Other ....

3.7 Were you told about the aims of the project when you first came?   **Y/N**

3.8 What did you want from the project when you came?

3.9 Have you got what you wanted   **Y/N**

3.10 Were/are any changes expected by another person as a result of your using the project?   **Y / N**

3.11 If Y, what were/are they?

....

....

3.12 Have these changes happened?
No   Partly   Yes

3.13 What services will you receive in the coming weeks or months from the project? ....

3.14 What do you hope these will achieve
For you? ....

For a child? ....

Other? ....

3.15 These are some possible functions of the project **for you**. Please tick those functions you think the project fulfils and also put the three most important for you in order (1 = *most important*)

  1. **A place to go away from home**
  2. **A place for the children**
  3. **A place to meet people**
  4. **A place to find out about what is going on in the neighbourhood**
  5. **A place to get practical help (eg a phone call)**
  6. **A place I can do some work to sort out my own problems**
  7. **A place where someone can help me**
  8. **A place to find out where to get what you need**
  9. **Other**

3.16 In your own words, what does the project mean to you? (a story)

MEASURES RELEVANT TO THE GENERATION AND RESOLUTION OF FAMILY PROBLEMS (ADAPTED FROM GIBBONS AND WILKINSON, 1990)

		Answer
1a)	How many children do you have?	N =
1b)	How many of these children are under 16 yrs old?	N =
1c)	How many of these children are under 5 yrs old?	N =
2a)	Are you a home-owner?	Y/N
2b)	Are you a council tenant? Or	
2c)	Do you privately rent an unfurnished flat?	Y/N
3a)	How many people live in your household (total of adults and children)?	N =
3b)	How many rooms to do you occupy?	N =
4)	Do you have the following	

a)	T.V.	Y/N
b)	Fridge	Y/N
c)	Washing machine	Y/N
d)	Car	Y/N
e)	Telephone	Y/N

5)	Is any one in your household currently working?	Y/N
6)	How old were you when you left school?	Age...... yrs
7)	Do you have any qualifications e.g. GCSE?	Y/N
8)	How old were you when your first child was born?	Age...yrs
9)	Are both parents living together?	Y/N
10)	How many moves have you had in the last five years?	N =
11)	Have you ever been a victim of violence?	Y/N
12)	As a child, were you ever harmed?	Y/N
13)	Has your child ever been subject of Child Protection enquiries/investigation/CPCC/CPR?	Y/N
14)	Have you, or has your partner, a criminal record?	Y/N

INDEX

Note: page references in *italics* refer to tables.